Write It Right:

Exercises to Unlock the Writer in Everyone

* * *

Workbook #1:

Units 1, 2, 3: Character, Setting, Story

By
Susan Tuttle

Write It Right:
Exercises to Unlock the Writer In Everyone
Unit 1: Character
Unit 2: Setting
Unit 3: Story

Susan's website and blog: www.SusanTuttleWrites.com
Email Susan at: aim2write@yahoo.com
Follow Susan on Twitter: @stuttleauthor, Facebook and LinkedIn

Cover design by: Aaron Kondziela (www.aaronkondziela.com)

A WriterWithin Publication
ISBN-10: 1941465021
ISBN-13: 978-1-941465-02-8

Write It Right:

Exercises to Unlock the Writer in Everyone

Workbook #1:

Units 1, 2, 3: Character, Setting, Story

Dedication

The first unit, **Character,** is dedicated to the members of my first *"What If?"* Writing Group, who have trusted me with two hours of their time every week on an on-going basis for over three years. Their enthusiasm, growth and encouragement inspired me to put these exercises into book format and make them available to writers everywhere. Every week this group reminds me how much I love teaching and mentoring writers of all levels.

So, a huge *Thank You!* to: Mark Arnold, Judythe Guarnera, Ginger Lasher, Anne Peterson, Lynne Diane Smith, Richard Sudden, Anna Unkovich and Dennis Eamon Young. Wonderful writers and characters, all.

To Debra Davis Hinkle, another terrific writer, whose friendship, generosity and digital expertise made it possible for you to hold this in your hands. From one cat lady to another: You're the best! (www.KritiqueKritics.com)

And to the "Mouse-behind-the-scenes," always there to make the unworkable work. We couldn't do it without you, Christine...

The second unit, **Setting**, is dedicated to my creative home, SLO NightWriters, the premier writing organization on the Central Coast of California (www.slonightwriters.org) None can compare. And to Anne Peterson, an amazing writer and one of the strongest women I know. She took a lonely East Coast transplant under her wing and introduced me to the Central Coast's writing community, and especially SLO NightWriters. And she taught me that it is okay to be who I am—no apologies necessary. Love you, Anne.

I'd also like to send a bushel of gratitude to my multi-talented son, Aaron Kondziela, (www.aaronkondziela.com) computer guru, musician, cinematographer and graphic artist, whose confidence in me has helped shape my writing career. From your critiques as I read my first chapters of the still-unfinished Norrak series to you when you were in sixth grade ("Too much character development, Mom!"), to teaching me the computer and designing my amazing book covers—Thank You, for your love and your honesty. And for believing in me long before I did.

Unit Three, **Story,** is dedicated to the writers who have inspired me with their ideas and their expertise in combining words into magnificent flights of fancy. I wanted to be you, and since I couldn't, I decided to try to write like you. And in the process I discovered my own voice. And myself.

Thank you to: Elizabeth George, Anne Perry, Orson Scott Card, Roger Zelazny, J.D. Robb, Patricia Cornwell, Tess Gerritson, Kathy Reichs, Isaac Asimov, Philip Wylie, Sir Arthur Conan Doyle, Ray Bradbury, Charles Dickens, Lisa Jackson, Sarah Paretsky, Janet Evanovich, Ruth Rendell, Lisa Gardner, Julie Garwood, Anne Rice, Elmore Leonard … the list goes on and on.

Contents

Before You Begin

YES, THERE'S THE USUAL here as you can see from the contents listing, all the front matter that most people simply skip. Unless, like me, you love to read every word in a book, even the boring technical stuff. But it's a good idea to at least skim the *Foreword*, because it details in brief the origin of this book and the validity of the exercises contained herein. The *Introduction* tells about the exercises and how they work, so you should definitely read that.

Also, please make sure to read *The Value of Timed Writing*, since the exercises depend on using that technique to complete them. A thorough understanding of how timed writing works will help you stick to the allotted time limits and make your learning process more effective and pleasurable.

And of course, don't skip the *Recommended Book List*. They are all invaluable resources for your writing library.

Foreword

WRITING IS MY LIFE. I have a thousand stories knocking on the inside of my head, seeking the freedom of paper. I also love to learn, especially about writing and ways to improve my range and skills. But I'm not very disciplined when it comes to how-to books. If it's not a mystery or suspense novel, I lose interest quickly, even if the subject matter is fascinating.

I've found that, for me, the best way to learn something is to teach it to someone else. I have a passion for writing, so I decided to start a group where I could teach what I wanted to learn. If nothing else, it would force me to read those "how to write" books I've been collecting.

So, I started the *What If?* Writing Group through SLO NightWriters on the Central Coast of California. I began with a group of six writers of various writing skills and genres, both fiction and creative nonfiction. We met once a week for two hours to explore in depth a specific aspect of fiction writing. I worried at first that, given the weekly commitment, the group would gradually peter out. But not only did they keep showing up, they started arranging appointments and planning trips around the lessons so they wouldn't miss any!

They kept coming and I kept researching, and eventually I ended up with 12 units full of lessons, enough for a full year at one or two a week. As the year began winding down, I wondered how to attract a new group of students. I had grown to love the teaching and wanted the *What If?* Writing Group to continue. Amazingly, when the year was up only one person left the group, and that was due to health problems. Everyone else wanted to repeat the course. We picked up three new members and started again from the beginning. I feared repeating the exercises would soon bore the original six. To my surprise, we discovered the exercises worked just as well as the first time around—and in some instances, even better. That was not what I expected would happen. It seems that, no matter where you are in your writing journey, or how many times you do these exercises, they continue to work. Every time.

I'm amazed at the growth I've seen in our group. A few are now getting published on a regular basis and are winning awards in writing contests. In fact, three of us won first place awards in different categories at the Central Coast Writers Conference in September of 2011. One even came home with three prizes in the competition! I believe the *What If?* Writing Group exercises have had a hand in unlocking the talent of every member of the group. To that end—and with a lot of urging and encouragement from *What If?* Writing Group members—I decided to collect all the lessons into a series of 12 instruction "units," divided into 6 workbooks. This workbook contains the first three units of the series: ***Character, Setting and Story.***

Introduction to Workbook #1

THIS COURSE GREW OUT of the writing lessons I designed for my *What If?* Writing Group, which I broke into the 12 skill areas all writers need to master. Each unit presents detailed explanations of the aspects of a particular skill, followed by writing exercises that will help you explore and learn these various aspects of each skill.

This volume, **Workbook #1**, contains the first three units: **Character, Setting and Story**. I grouped these together because to me these are the three basic skills every writer needs. Without believable characters, fascinating settings and an intriguing idea, you don't have anything worth writing. An asterisk on the lesson title means there's an example at the end of the unit from the writing that I do in my classes. They're there just in case you need clarification of a particular lesson or point.

With most of the lessons, I also reference the books I used to formulate the lessons and exercises (along with their publication dates, because some have published newer editions than the ones I have), great books for all writers to have in their personal writing libraries. You don't need to read the recommended pages in those books to use this course, but doing so will add to the depth of your experience.

It doesn't matter what level you are: beginner, intermediate or advanced. These exercises **cross boundaries** and address where you are now in your writing career—and get you to where you want to be.

Also, these are **not** time-intensive sessions. You only need to dedicate approximately 30-45 minutes to each of these activities, though a few may take up to an hour or more. There are **26 exercises total** in this first Workbook, contained in the units that reference the specific technique you need to master. If you do two exercises a week, it will take you just over three months to finish all the exercises. There's no time limit here; feel free to move at your own pace—one or two exercises a week, or every two weeks. Or even once a month. But if you choose a fast-track pace, do give yourself enough time assimilate each lesson. It's best to have a couple of days between each exercise. (The *What If?* Writing Group does one or two exercises per session, with a week between sessions.)

The exercises in each unit are designed pull out your innate talent, strengthen your confidence and teach you strategies to solve character and plot problems. There is a full listing of all the volumes of the **Write It Right** series at the end of the Workbook.

Since this volume is designed as a workbook, you can fill in the pages (though you will need extra paper to finish most of the exercises) as you work through the lessons. But I recommend that you use separate sheets of paper, a notebook, or work digitally in a word processing program, so that when you return to the lessons as you feel the need or the desire, you won't be distracted by your previous answers to the lesson questions.

All you need is a timer and something to write with—pen (or pencil) and paper, or computer and keyboard, whichever is most comfortable for you, and a timer you can set in minute increments. For maximum results, you might want to pick up a copy of some of the books I've used to formulate these lessons, and which I will reference throughout the course. As I noted above, it's not necessary, though it will broaden your understanding some of the concepts.

As you explore and hone your skills you'll see remarkable changes in your writing, and in your understanding of what it means to be a writer. But remember, it's an ongoing process. Writing is a dynamic art and like life it's a journey through which you are always growing and learning. Over time your writing will expand to reflect your continuing life experiences and the skills you learn. Celebrate the journey. It's time to get started.

The Value of Timed Writing

MOST OF THE EXERCISES in this course are timed. You have a specified amount of time to complete each one, usually 15 or 20 minutes. You set the timer, write until it dings and then stop. That's it. Period.

Why timed writing? There are two major benefits to time-limited sessions. As *Natalie Goldman* shows in *Writing Down The Bones*, timed writing exercises force you to keep writing. You have a specific goal and only a short time in which to accomplish it. You have to step out of your way, turn off your inner editor—who is constantly telling you you've used the wrong word, no one will believe that plot, your characters aren't "real" enough, etc.—and simply write. From your heart, from your subconscious instincts, from the place where your stories live. It's authentic writing that's scraped to the bone of emotion. It's the kind of compelling writing that makes readers want more.

The second benefit is that you learn to **trust yourself and your writing process**. When we learn to put our conscious mind on hold and just let the words flow, amazing things happen. Stories emerge that we never knew were there. Connections get made that our conscious minds would never have considered. Best of all, our authentic voice emerges, announcing in clear, ringing tones, "This is who I am as a writer. This is what I need to say. This is the way I need to say it." Timed writing exercises will introduce you to yourself.

Timed exercises allow you to step away from your editor self and into your writer self because you don't have time to think. You have to just keep writing, no matter what comes out. It may be hard at first not to go back and correct that word, rethink that action, direct the flow, etc. It takes time to learn to trust your instincts. When you find yourself wanting to go back and "fix it," don't. *Write* about wanting to go back to fix it until you return to the natural flow of the exercise. You can always cut out the extraneous parts later. That's what editing is for.

Timed Writing Format "Rules"

Read the lesson, make sure you understand what to do, then set your timer and write until it dings. Don't stop to think, don't edit as you go, just keep your pen or pencil moving or your fingers typing on the keyboard. If you can't think of anything at first, write about not being able to think of anything and just see what happens. Repeat for the next lesson. And the next, and the next...

Also, be aware that my use of the terms "character," "person," "people," "he" and "she" are meant to indicate the protagonists, antagonists and other characters in your stories, whether they be humans, animals or otherworldly creatures. Make whatever adjustments you need to make so each exercise fits your specific genre and character choice.

Note: An asterisk on the title of an exercise denotes that there is an example of that exercise from my own writing at the end of the section.

32 23333

Recommended Book List

THESE BOOKS, AMONG OTHERS, have been instrumental in the formation of these lessons. Throughout the course I will reference the pertinent page or pages to read in the appropriate volume. Although you don't need these books to complete the lessons, the information they contain is invaluable. It will add to your knowledge and skills and enhance your learning throughout this series. And they will form a solid foundation for your writer's reference library.

I am listing the copyright year for each volume, so that if you want to read the suggested pages, you will have the correct volume in which to find them. How-to books are often updated with new examples and insights. If you obtain a volume published after the dates listed below, you will still get the same fantastic writing information. But because things will have shifted around in newer editions, you might have trouble finding the proper references for each lesson unless you use a volume with the same publication date as those listed below.

Write Away by Elizabeth George (2004)

What If? Writing Exercises for Writers by Anne Bernays and Pamela Painter (1990)

On Writing by Stephen King (2000)

Characters & Viewpoint by Orson Scott Card (1988)

How to Write a Damn Good Novel by James N. Frey (1987)

The Novel Writer's Toolkit by Bob Mayer (2003)

Finding Your Writer's Voice: A Guide to Creative Fiction by Thaisa Frank and Dorothy Wall (1994)

The 38 Most Common Fiction Writing Mistakes and How to Avoid Them by Jack M. Bickham (1992)

Make A Scene by Jordan Rosenfeld (2008)

And every writer's library should contain the following reference volumes:

***The biggest dictionary** you can afford (check used bookstores for bargains). There's no substitute for a good, print dictionary

**Roget's Thesaurus*

**Sisson's Synonms* (if you can find it)

**The Elements of Style* (Strunk and White)

**Barron's Essentials of English*

Unit 1: Character

"Plot springs from character... I've always sort of believed that these people inside me—these characters—know who they are and what they're about and what happens, and they need me to help get it down on paper because they don't type."

~Anne Lamott

HAVE YOU EVER READ a book, been totally immersed in the story, identified with the character and then—the character said or did something totally out of character, completely unbelievable? And there went your enjoyment. If you kept reading, you started to question everything. You saw the pattern behind the writing. You could no longer lose sight of the fact that it is merely a story. It's fiction. It's not real.

That happens because the writer does not know his characters. Not completely. Though he probably thinks he does. If you question him about it, he'll say, "Of course I know my characters!" But why, then, did the character say or do something that wasn't believable?

Knowing your characters even **better than you know yourself** is the key to creating consistently believable people for your stories. Here are **9 intensive exercises** designed to help you get to the "heart and soul" of each of your characters.

Unit 1, Character: Contents

Lesson #1: Creating Characters

WHAT IS A STORY? A story is character. It's people, animals, alien beings, whoever your protagonists are. Sounds simplistic, I know, but think about it.

A volcano blows up. A fire rages across the land. A tsunami engulfs the coast for three miles inland. Great headlines, but those aren't stories. They are events that catch our attention for just a few moments. Not until living beings are involved and threatened in some way, or are given monumental challenges to overcome, do we have potential tragedy looming on the horizon. The characters have the opportunity to learn and grow, to gain a deeper understanding of life, to help someone else or make the world a little better place in which to live. And now we have a story.

When readers feel a **connection** to a story's characters they empathize with them, and they have to know what happens. They turn the page, then the next and the next, living the events and learning vicariously through the characters.

Creating compelling characters entails knowing each and every character in our stories as well as—and in the case of the main characters, perhaps even better than—we know ourselves. We **must** know what our characters will do **in every circumstance**. Not just within the limits of the story, but also beyond it. What would they do if they actually were alive and living in the real world? If our characters are not that real to us, how then can they be real enough for our readers to care about them?

Too often we begin a story with only **a vague idea** of who our main characters are. We have a mere glimmer of the kind of person she is, or what he might do if confronted with a certain choice. A specific personality or quirk, or an unusual choice made by someone we know or hear about, might be what sparks the story idea itself. But to succeed as a believable story, we must then create fully developed, believable people to populate the events that occur. One huge reason writers can become bogged down in the middle of a story is that they don't know the characters well enough to know what they would do, or how they would react to the various story events.

HERE ARE THE RULES: When you are given specifics, such as an opening sentence or phrase, use them. There are definite reasons for the structure of each exercise. Read the directions carefully to make sure you understand what you are to do. Then, **once you start to write, don't stop** to think or plan. Keep your pen or pencil moving across the paper or your fingers typing on the keyboard. If you can't think of what to write, write that you can't think of anything and keep going from there. The important thing is to **keep writing, no matter what,** for the allotted time.

Trust your inner instincts to keep the character's voice true as he/ she tells about his/her childhood and/or family. Let the character speak through you. Don't try to force or direct the information. Let the character reveal him-/herself to you as you write. Don't stop to think. Turn off your inner editor. Just let the words flow and see what happens.

READ: *Write Away* (George, 2004) Page 4, starting with the 2nd paragraph, to Page 5, ending after the second paragraph.

*Exercise #1: Creating a Character**

(Purpose of Exercise: To learn to trust our inner character-creating instincts and to ignore our inner editor)

Pick an Age (circle one):

7   13   18   23   27   31   36   44   49   52   58   66   68   75   89

Pick an Eye Color: _____

Pick a Hair Color: _____

Name of City or Town (real or imagined): _____

Type of Residence or House: _____

Create a Name using these Initials:

    First Name: G _____

    Last Name: F _____

Choose a Prominent Facial or Body Feature: _____

_____

Choose a Passion for this Character: _____

_____

Pick a Weird Quirk for this Character: _____

_____

Pick the Gender: Male _____ Female _____

Set your timer for **20 MINUTES** and write until the timer dings. Don't stop to think or second-guess yourself. Now become this character. **Write about this character's family or childhood**, starting with the following opening sentence:

Nothing ever worked out the way I hope it would when...

Lesson #2: Writing the Opposite Gender

CREATING A CHARACTER WHO is the same sex as ourselves is fairly easy, especially if the character has had a similar upbringing and education. But stories are not populated only by people like us. Some stories might have no one who is like us in them. Men must learn to write convincingly about women. Women must write believable men. Twenty-year-olds must be able to create compelling eighty-year-olds. Eighty-year-olds might need a believable thirteen-year-old character. Well-educated writers sometimes need to create poorly educated characters, and vice versa. We may need to create a character whose culture or religious beliefs are totally different from ours. Our stories will need as wide a variety of characters as we find in real life. And every one of them needs to be well-rounded and believable to the reader.

The same timed-writing rules apply: Read the exercise carefully to make sure you understand what you are to do. Then once you start to write, don't stop to think or plan. Keep your pen/pencil moving across the paper, your fingers typing on the keyboard. If you can't think of what to write, write that you can't think of anything, and why, and see what happens. The important thing is to **keep writing, no matter what, for the allotted time.**

READ: *What If?* (Bernays & Painter, 1990) Page 37

Exercise #2: Writing the Opposite Gender

(Purpose of Exercise: To learn to create characters who are completely different from ourselves.)

WRITE IN THE VOICE of someone who is totally different from you. If you are a man, write as a woman. If you are a woman, become a man for this exercise. The point of the exercise is to **lose yourself in the character**, to learn to write well-rounded, believable, sympathetic characters who are completely different from you, even if you don't particularly like them or admire them.

What you write can be a diatribe, a journal entry, a reminiscence, a segment of an autobiography, a description, etc., as long as it's **in the character's voice and reflects the character's thoughts and beliefs.** It can be in first or third person. Check to make sure you have clear identifying characteristics for your character: cadence of speech; bias of opinion; choice of language; philosophy of life; race, age, gender; educational level, etc. All those things go into the makeup of the character, and make him/her real to the reader. Put it all in this exercise.

Set your timer for 20 MINUTES and write until the buzzer goes off.

Lesson #3: Understanding Your Characters

THINK YOU KNOW YOUR characters now? There's a very interesting and fun way to discover just how well you do know your characters. You might be surprised at what you find out about them—and even discover that you don't yet know them as well as you think you do.

Have you ever been surprised at what a character did or said in your story? Have you ever looked at what you wrote and thought, *I never intended him to say that*, or, *I hadn't planned for her to do that?* When characters become real they will seem to take over your story. Then surprising things come out in the writing.

No, you're not going crazy. You, the writer, are still in control. It's just your subconscious instincts coming to the fore. The more you identify with your characters, the better you know them, the more your inner intuition will steer the writing, keeping your characters' personalities honest and consistent.

Often your conscious awareness of who your characters are is not as clear as your subconscious awareness, and sometimes your story will veer off in a direction you hadn't intended. It will feel like a muddle. But if you've done your "character homework" and truly know your characters, when this happens it will actually enhance the story instead of stopping it dead. Often these "muddles" result in surprising and unique twists you hadn't consciously considered.

So, how do you get to know your characters that well? Try this: Become the character and take a standard personality test **as that character** (there are plenty online, and you can start with my version in Exercise #3). It will give you a deep insight into the inner workings of each character's mind. It will help you understand why the character does what he does, says what she says—and refuses to do or say what you want them to at times. You just might be surprised at who your character really is. When you know your characters that deeply, that knowledge will help keep you on track in rendering them for the reader.

If you're having trouble connecting with your character when taking the test—if you find yourself answering the way you would answer rather than the way the character would—here's a hint that helps my students. Take the personality test as yourself, first, then become the character and take it again. Doing it both ways can help you disconnect your personal responses from those of your character.

READ: *On Writing* (King, 2000) Page 188 from #8 to Page 190 through last full paragraph on the page.

Exercise #3: Characters—Who Are They?

(Purpose of Exercise: To understand the deep, inner workings of our characters.)

USE A CHARACTER FROM a story you are working on or thinking about writing (not a story you have already finished). It can be one of the protagonists, the antagonist, the sidekick, anyone who is not a minor character in the story. Consider the character's basic need in the story (ex: In *The Wizard of Oz*, Dorothy's need is to get back to Kansas) and the character's role—or potential role if the story isn't yet started—in the story. (For example, Dorothy is the main female protagonist.) Fill in the following information about the character:

Character's Name: _____

Character's Basic Need in the Story:_____

_____

Character's (Potential) Role in the Story:_____

_____

Now, set your timer for **10 MINUTES** and take the following personality test *as if you are the character.* Try to choose answers the character would choose depending on the character's own personality and life style. Trust your instincts here. **Don't second-guess your**

answers. Your first response is probably the right one. Besides, you only have ten minutes to finish the test!

Sample Personality Test to Use For Your Characters

I work best:

>A) In large groups
>
>B) In small groups
>
>C) By myself

I would choose a job that:

>A) Is stable and financially secure
>
>B) Offers variety and travel although slightly unstable or insecure
>
>C) Is full of adventure and danger and totally insecure

My emotional response is usually:

>A) Not often affected by my mood swings
>
>B) Varied depending on my mood at the time

For me, it's important to:

>A) Understand my feelings and how they affect me
>
>B) Move on and not spend time thinking about myself

If I were a garden I would most likely be:

>A) A Wildflower garden — exuberant, carefree and outgoing
>
>B) An English Garden — organized and precise
>
>C) A Cactus Garden — prickly, isolated, efficient

I trust strangers:

    A) Easily, most people are basically trustworthy;

    B) Not easily, trust needs to be earned

When my surroundings are cluttered, I:

    A) Have to neaten things up

    B) Am not really bothered by it

    C) Let stuff pile up and then marathon clean

Debates of a philosophical nature (ie, the meaning of the universe) interest me:

    A) A whole lot

    B) Not much at all

In general I am:

    A) More into facts than speculation

    B) More into speculation than facts

When I need to make a decision, I:

    A) Am impulsive and choose fast

    B) Take time to analyze my options

    C) Am indecisive and can't decide without help

I am most interested in:

    A) Causes (what created the situation)

    B) Effects (what was the result of the situation)

    C) Relationships (how this situation connects to other situations)

When assessing other people, I generally:

A) Can explain my conclusions rationally

B) Rely my gut feelings that I can't put into words

It is more true that I:

A) Should spend more time worrying about problems

B) Shouldn't spend so much time worrying about problems

A hallway in a friend's apartment has been redecorated. You:

A) Don't notice because your attention is elsewhere

B) Notice but don't care all that much

C) Notice and take in all the details

You are invited to go bungee jumping. You say:

A) Yes, and are immediately excited

B) Probably, and are scared but interested

C) Maybe not, but will think about it

D) No way, you'll cheer from the ground

Scale of 1-100, what percentage of your personal potential are you living right now:

1-14; 15-24; 25-34; 35-44; 45-54; 55-64; 65-74; 75-84; 85-94; 95-100%

I enjoy entertaining, gathering friends, organizing get-togethers:

A) Not often/not particularly

B) Occasionally

C) Fairly often

D) Very often/regularly

What would you change about yourself:

    A) Stubbornness

    B) Impulsivity (acting without thinking)

    C) Tendency to worry/be anxious

    D) Indecisiveness (can't make up mind)

    E) Lack of discipline/organization

    F) Lack of spontaneity/ too organized

    G) Lack of ambition (not too motivated)

    H) Over-ambition (work too much)

    I) Overly sensitive

Choose **one** from **each pair:**

    A) busy/rushing — Calm, quiet

    B) Reality — Imagination

    C) Stability — Flexibility

    D) Outspoken — Reserved

    E) Be praises — Get a prize

    F) Complex/abstract — Simple/ concrete

When it comes to responsibility, I:

    A) Take it lightly—call me a free spirit

    B) Sometimes do it right

    C) Am pretty good at handling it

    D) Am very responsible

In my free time I:

    A) Like to be relaxed and not active

    B) Am more relaxed than active

C) Am more active than relaxed

D) Like to be on the go

In an average week, I make people around me laugh:

A) Not much, I don't do humor

B) Occasionally

C) Fairly often

D) Often/regularly

Being the best in my field is:

A) Not important to me

B) Slightly important

C) Moderately important

D) Very important

I tell those for whom I have strong feelings how I feel about them:

A) Rarely—I don't show my feelings

B) Occasionally

C) Often

D) Very often—I'm quite affectionate

Someone cuts in front of me in line. I find this:

A) No big deal

B) Rather annoying

C) Annoying

D) Unbelievably annoying

Not knowing if the person did this on purpose, do I tell them to move to the back of the line:

Yes_____   No _____

Most of the chaos in my life is caused by:
    A) Others, Im never to blame
    B) Other people most of the time
    C) Sometimes me
    D) Me, I'm always to blame

Me and high stress:
    A) Don't get along, it knocks me down every time
    B) Sometimes I handle it okay
    C) Have a working relationship most of the time
    D) Work together like clockwork

On the issues of the day, I consider myself:
    A) Conservative
    B) Moderate
    C) Liberal

Math and math stuff interests me:
    A) Not at all
    B) A little bit
    C) Somewhat
    D) Very much

Once I have my mind made up I will seldom change it:

    A) Very true, I believe what I believe

    B) Pretty true of me

    C) Not too true of me

    D) Not true of me, I'm open to differing opinions

I would rather be:

    A) A logical person who can reason clearly

    B) A compassionate person who is understanding/empathetic

How important is it to help humans and animals who are deprived:

    A) Somewhat

    B) Quite

    C) Very

    D) Extremely

I believe emotional closeness needs to come before sexual intimacy:

    A) Not at all

    B) A little bit

    C) To some extent

    D) To a great extent

    E) To a very great extent

I am jealous:

    A) Fairly often

    B) Occasionally

    C) Sometimes, but not very often

    D) Rarely, it's not my style

My attitude toward marital sexual roles is:

    A) Traditional

    B) Mostly traditional

    C) Mixed

    D) Mostly nontraditional

    E) Very nontraditional

When it comes to work, I:

    A) Need exact directions

    B) Finish what I work on

    C) Do more than one thing at a time

    D) Do only one thing at a time

    E) Follow my own path

    F) Get someone else to finish it

    G) Am a self-starter

    H) Need constant supervision

Rate **each** of these from 1 (not much) to 5 (very much)

I am:

  Romantic

  Organized

  Playful

  Assertive (speak my mind)

  Nurturing (a caregiver)

  Outgoing/socially active

  Able to criticize others without feeling uneasy

  Tend to fill the dominant role when working in a group

Consider arguing a sport

Prefer to be friends with assertive people

Long-term partnership relationships: (same scale as above)

   The ideal partner should be:

      Assertive

      Nurturing

      Socially outgoing

      Dominant in a group

When you finish taking the personality test **as your character,** look at your answers and analyze the results for patterns of behavior and thought, etc. Is your character a loner or a party animal? Or somewhere in between? Is she meticulous or sloppy, does he wear his heart on his sleeve or hide his feelings, is she intuitive or concrete? Does he have a strong spiritual base, or does he go through life on his own? And so on.

Figure out just who this person is in his/her deepest inner recesses. What makes this character tick? Consider whether this character has a pessimistic or optimistic outlook on life. Who is this person when this person is all alone, not looking to impress anyone?

Now **set your timer for 15 MINUTES** and write about the character, starting with:

(Name) is the sort of person who_____

_____

_____

_____

_____

_____

_____

_____.

This is a great exercise to do for **all your main characters**, and even the incidental—but still important—ones like the protagonist's sidekick, the antagonist's foil, important family members and friends, etc. It can reveal layers you weren't aware of, and lead to fabulous subplots that add excitement and complications to your stories.

Lesson #4: If I Were A...

IN ORDER TO MAKE characters interesting to the reader, you first must make the characters interesting to you. After all, you are going to spend a lot of time with these paper people. Why be bored by them? Remember, if they bore you, they will probably also make your readers yawn.

An interesting way to learn more about your characters, and even discover some of their quirks, is to make them other than people. We all know people who are as meek as a lamb, as fierce as a tiger, as wise as an owl (to string together a bunch of cliches). Now consider this: **If your character weren't a person, who or what would that person be?** And can any of those other "identities," if you will, lead to fascinating quirks, body images, or threatening weaknesses?

A person's quirks and/or weaknesses make them interesting. No one would want to be around someone who is perfect, not for very long —even super heroes have a foot or two of clay in their makeup. The following exercise will not only help you understand your character better, but can also help you find some of those fascinating quirks and/or weaknesses that will make your character compelling to the reader.

READ: *Character and Viewpoint* (Card, 1998), "You Are The First Audience," Pages 15-17.

Exercise #4: Character: If I Were A... I'd Be A...*

(Purpose of Exercise: To more completely understand who your characters are and find interesting idiosyncrasies to make them more well-rounded)

HOW WELL DO YOU really know your character(s)? Consider the following in regard to the character you worked with in the last exercise. Choose the most appropriate answer for each question, then **explain why you chose that answer.** Give yourself **15 MINUTES** to complete this exercise.

If my character were a _____, he/she would be a _____ because ____.

Animal: _____, because:_____

_____

Mode of Transportation: _____, because:_____

_____

Dwelling: _____, because:_____

_____

Garden Type: _____, because:_____

_____

Vegetable: _____, because:_____

_____

Weather Pattern: _____, because:_____

_____

TV Program: _____, because:_____

_____

Article of Clothing: _____, because:_____

_____

Type of Footwear: _____, because:_____

_____

Day of the Week: _____, because:_____

_____

Type of Music: _____, because:_____

_____

Piece of Furniture: _____, because:_____

_____

Geographical Formation: _____, because:_____

_____

Religion: _____, because:_____

_____

Tree: _____, because:_____

_____

Corporation: _____, because:_____

_____

Knick-Knack: _____, because:_____

_____

Book: _____, because:_____

_____

Painting: _____, because:_____

_____

Movie: _____, because:_____

_____

Type of Money: _____, because:_____

_____

Sculpture: _____, because:_____

_____

Type of Lamp: _____, because:_____

_____

Fruit: _____, because:_____

_____

Sports Equipment: _____, because:_____

_____

Personal Care Product:_____, because:_____

_____

Kind of Dinnerware:_____, because:_____

_____

$\mathcal{L}$esson #5: Your Character's Bio

A GOOD HABIT TO cultivate is writing a biographical sketch for **each** of your characters. Not only does this help you to keep the characters' physical descriptions straight, it also helps you know the characters intimately. And it provides a handy reference of details you can check while you are writing the story, so John's eyes are not blue in chapter three and green in chapter twenty, Sarah doesn't shrink from 5'9" to 5'5" as the story progresses, and Edwin doesn't start out at Yale and graduate from Princeton without switching schools. (I just read a book where one character threw a vase, and later other characters talked about the lamp that he threw.)

Just as the people we meet have pasts that have worked to shape who they are and how they view and react to the world around them, so do our characters have lives independent of the story in which they appear. They were born into a family of some sort, grew up, went to school, got a job, got married, got divorced, had children, had affairs, own homes and cars, have hobbies and passions, etc. **Everything that happened to them before the story begins helped shape who they are**

and how they will react to the story events. Knowing a character's full background helps you create well-rounded, interesting characters with whom your readers can connect.

Another reason to thoroughly know your characters' backgrounds is that often something in a character's past can trigger a subplot in the story that adds depth, interest and excitement. The best subplots will arise naturally from the characters' motivations and lives, and weave seamlessly into the main plot. A good, detailed character biography is a great hunting ground for such subplot sparkers.

READ: *What If?* (Bernays & Painter) Page 46; and *Write Away* (George) Page 216-218

Exercise #5: Creating a Character Bio

(Purpose of Exercise: To create a full life for your character before the story begins.)

CHOOSE A COMPLETED STORY, or one you are in the process of completing, and work with a character who you think you know well. Or choose a character that still needs fleshing out to appear more real. Now fill in the blanks and see how well you really do know your character(s). As you answer, **ask yourself why:** Why is this the character's nickname; why are these the character's superstitions? **Write down your answers**.

Give yourself **20 MINUTES** to complete this biography. Add as much detail and explanation to your answers as you can. (Many thanks to writer Sharyl Heber for adding some great items to the listing.)

Story title

Character's Name

Gender

Character's Nickname

Age

Physical description

Education

Vocation/Occupation

Status/Money

Marital Status

Close Family

Extended Family

Ethnicity

Diction, accent, etc.

Relationships with family

Relationships with friends

Enemies

Resides (name of town/city)

Lives in (type of building)

Works in

Type of vehicle driven

Favorite Possession(s)

Favorite Sport(s)

Obsessions

Political Beliefs

Philosophy of life

Sexual History

Ambitions

Religion/religious beliefs

Superstitions

Fears

Attitudes

Character Flaw(s)

Character Strengths

Pets

Taste in Music, Books, TV, Movies, etc.

Journal Entries

Hobbies

Memberships

Correspondence

Food Preferences (favorites, most hated, etc)

Handwriting

Astrological Sign

Talents

Most Embarrassing Moment

Happiest Moment

Alcohol Consumption

Drug Use

Health issues

Mental Stability

Future Plans

Any other information you can think of about this character

Lesson #6: Characters and Their Desires

PEOPLE DON'T DO THINGS just to do them. They have reasons for everything they do—and don't do—whether they are conscious of those reasons or not.

Just as in real life, our story characters cannot do things just because we want them to do so, or because we need a specific thing to happen to move the plot along. The easiest way to lose a reader is to have a character act "out of character."

We've all read books where we did not believe that a particular character would do what he just did, or would say what she just said. Didn't that ruin the story for you? Perhaps, like me, you didn't bother to finish the book, because you just couldn't enjoy or believe the story anymore. And, like me, you probably never read anything else that author wrote.

Our characters must always act "in character" or we will lose our readers' trust. They are giving us hours of their precious time, and trusting that the story we give in return will not waste those hours. They are leaving their lives behind, suspending disbelief and entering a world we have created for them. All they ask in return is **a compelling story that is consistent and believable.** When we break that trust, we lose our readers, often forever.

To make sure we don't have our characters doing and saying unbelievable things, we have to know their desires. We must be clear on what each character wants, his or her main desire in life. One character may want to be successful no matter what he must do. Another may want revenge for a wrong committed against her in childhood. Another may seek approval through helping others. And so on.

These main desires are the driving forces that impel our characters to choose between good and evil, right and wrong, good and bad. This main desire shapes their lives—the way they think, the way they speak, the way they act. And knowing your characters' main desires can help you avoid making them wimpy, or unable to act. Wimpy characters are boring to readers. They want characters who will act, especially if they are undecided or scared or doubtful.

Knowing a character's main desire is one key to creating a fully rounded, believable person who the reader will want to continue reading about. When our characters act within their main desires, the reader is right there with them, urging them on, rooting for them. When the character acts against his or her desire, it pulls the reader out of the story and kills the enjoyment. We've lost our reader. And that is something no writer ever wants to happen.

READ: *How To Write A Damn Good Novel* (Frey, 1987) section titled: "Creating Wonderfully Rounded Characters," Page 5-7; *What If?* (Bernays & Painter, 1990) Page 49-51; and *The 38 Most Common*

Mistakes (Bickham, 1992) Page 22 from 3rd paragraph to Page 23, ending after "And you have a story underway."

*Exercise #6: Characters and Their Desires**

(Purpose of Exercise: To understand the character's main life goal and how it affects his or her life choices.)

THE FOLLOWING EXERCISE COMES in **two parts**. Give yourself **10 minutes to complete Part A,** which explores your character's main life goal in the story. Then take **20 minutes to complete Part B**, which explores how that main life goal affects how your character would react to three other, random situations.

When you finish with this character, you might want to do this exercise with the other characters from your story.

Part A (10 MINUTES): Use the character from the last exercise and the story in which he or she appears. Answer the following questions about your character's main desire:

1) What does your character want?

2) What are the motives for your character wanting this?

3) Where in the story is (or will) this desire be made clear to the reader?

4) We learn what the character wants in three ways: through dialogue, action and interior thinking. To keep your story from being static (even too much action can pall after a while), make sure the story isn't too heavily weighted toward one form over the others. Fill in the

percentage of desire that will be revealed in your story through these three means:

        a) Dialogue: _____% and in what way?

        b) Action(s): _____% and what kind?

        c) Interior Thinking: _____% and how will it be integrated into the story?**

    5) What or who stands in the way of your character achieving this main desire?

    6) What action(s)/plot twist(s) does (or might) that desire set in motion?

    (**An example of this is what I wrote for my main protagonist in the paranormal detective series I am working on: Skylark's main desire is to solve the mystery because in the solution to mysteries of any kind lie the threads that might lead her to who she is and where she belongs. In this first story, how do we learn what she wants? What I envision at this point will be about 35% dialogue [scenes with the father of a young boy], 25% interior thoughts [self-questioning and doubts throughout the story] and 40% action [finding and revealing the true perpetrators of the crime].)

    Give yourself **10 MINUTES** to complete this part. Then go on to Part B.

Part B (20 MINUTES): Imagine that your character finds him or herself in **each of these ethical dilemmas.** Write a short, thorough scene for each one that taps into your character's thoughts, feelings, fears, conflicts and ultimately shows how your character arrives at the final decision or action. Keep them short, you only have **20 MINUTES** to complete **all three**.

A) Your character was offered a huge promotion or large bonus for a project your character did not carry out alone. Does your character speak up or keep all the glory for him/herself? Why?

B) Your character returns from grocery shopping to discover that a bag of expensive meats from the customer ahead in line was inadvertently put into your character's cart. Does your character keep the groceries or return them to the store? Why?

C) Your character finds a wallet on the sidewalk containing full ID, credit cards and almost $1,000.00 in cash. Does your character return the wallet intact, return the wallet minus the cash, or keep the cash and throw the wallet away? Or do something else entirely? What and why?

Lesson #7: What's In A Name?

CHARACTER NAMES ARE VERY important. If your readers cannot connect with your characters' names, they won't engage in the story. Take my newly released suspense novel, *Proof of Identity*, for example. When writing it, I heard criticism from all my beta readers about the female protagonist's name. No one liked it, and no one could identify with the character because of it. When I changed her name to something more appropriate to the character's personality, all objections vanished. Readers now love the character, and **the only change was her name.**

The moral of the story? **Names Count!** If a character's name stands in the way, the reader won't believe the character would do or say certain things. They won't identify with the character, won't care about the character, and will stop reading. There is a definite reason Superman's name was not Jimmy Olson, and Hannibal Lechter was not saddled with the moniker Bill Smith.

READ: *What If?* (Bernays & Painter, 1990) Page 42; and *Write Away* (George, 2004), Page 7, starting with the last full paragraph on the page, to Page 8 to the end of the 2nd full paragraph.

Exercise #7: Naming Your Characters

(Purpose of Exercise: to practice finding appropriate names for your characters)

SET YOUR TIMER FOR **20 MINUTES**. Give the following characters names that you feel reflect who they are, **then explain your reasoning:**

1) A petty, white-collar thief who robs his boss over several years.

2) An envious bitter woman who makes her sister miserable by systematically trying to undercut her pleasure and self-confidence.

3) A sweet young man too shy to speak to a young woman he sees every day at work.

4) The owner of a fast-food restaurant who comes on to his female employees.

5) A grandmother who just won the lottery.

6) A bank teller who cowers in fear during a robbery.

7) The principal of an exclusive high school who stands up to bullying parents.

8) The class bully.

9) The class clown.

10) A supermarket checkout clerk who is always joking with customers.

11) A cop who gives drivers a ticket for going 2 miles over the speed limit.

12) A mild mannered accountant who spends his nights seeking vigilante justice.

13) The pastor of a small church in a small town whose main goal is to gather more parishioners.

14) The pastor of a huge church in a large city whose main goal is to become famous.

15) An honest politician (I know, it's an oxymoron, but work with me, here…)

16) A lawyer who leaves the DA's office to work for Legal Aid.

17) A lawyer who leaves Legal Aid to open a criminal defense firm.

18) A firefighter who is a secret arsonist.

19) A graduate English professor who lives in a fantasy world created from romance novels.

20) A used car salesman who wants to be successful but has a conscience.

21) A house painter who is highly meticulous.

22) A house painter who is a slob.

23) A bank manager who is severely dyslexic.

24) A pastor who does not believe in God.

25) A writer who thinks agents are out to get him/her.

26) A heroine who is brave but foolish.

27) A hero who believes he is a coward but does brave things.

28) A street tough who shoots out streetlights.

29) A law officer who can't follow rules or orders.

30) Now name **YOUR** Character and **tell why you chose that name:**

_____

_____

_____

_____.

Lesson #8: Private Spaces

THERE ARE MANY THINGS that reveal who we are: the clothes we wear, the food we eat, the type of automobile we drive, the books we read, our hobbies, our beliefs. One of the most revealing aspects of our lives is the place where we live.

Our home is the one place where we can be just ourselves, not what someone else expects us to be. And as such, we fill it with things that reveal who we are. We may collect teacups or angels, stamps or coins. We might quilt, sew or embroider. We might have a music studio of sorts set up in a corner of the living room. We may have dedicated a wall to the movie CDs we've purchased. We may be obsessively neat or a total slob. All these things are subtle, and at times not-so-subtle, clues to who we really are, especially when no one else is around.

Knowing the kind of place where our characters live and how they furnish this private space can give not only us as writers insight into who they are, but also clue in the reader. Private spaces can show a character's weaknesses and strengths and let the reader know what is most important to the character. A character's private space can reveal his or her core values, or reflect the conflicts with which the character is struggling.

Furnished by a thoughtful writer, a character's private space can also give clues as to future story events, or stand as metaphors to the character's life and/or transformation. Even if this private space is never used in the story itself, what it reveals to you about the character can be of monumental help in creating a compelling character and an unforgettable story.

READ: *What If?* (Bernays & Painter, 1990) Page 52, first paragraph.

*Exercise #8: A Character's Private Space**

(Purpose of Exercise: To help you visualize your characters in concrete terms.)

CREATE A PRIVATE SPACE for one of the following characters and furnish it to reveal his or her character. The reader must be able to see the character through **observation of the setting only.** The place can be any kind of locale: a house, a specific room in a house, outdoor grounds, an office, a cell or even a bed, a tent or a cardboard box, as long as it is that character's private space. The description must incorporate enough characteristic things so that the reader can accurately visualize the character and uncover clues to who this person is.

Avoid stereotypes, such as an easel with an unfinished painting in an artist's room. Think carefully and be specific in your choices. The right details reveal a lot about a character. Pick a character from the list below. Then time yourself for **15 MINUTES** as you write to create a private space for your chosen character.

Character Listing

1) An unsuccessful investment counselor
2) A once-notable writer who thinks she's still famous
3) A Ph.D. candidate about to flunk out
4) A shoe salesperson down on his luck
5) Someone who's deaf or blind
6) A paraplegic who lives alone
7) A member of a fanatical fringe religious group
8) A foster child
9) A cat burglar
10) A newly-rich social climber
11) Someone who's paranoid
12) An illegal factory worker who just won the state lottery

When you have finished, **RESET the timer for 15 MINUTES** and create a private setting for one of **your characters.**

Your Character: _____

Your Character' Room: _____

_____

_____

_____

_____

Lesson #9: Character As Setting

ONE OF THE MOST interesting ways to reveal who your character is deep inside is to look at that character from a different viewpoint—not as a person but **as a setting**. This is similar to Exercise #4, where we compared our character to many different things. But it goes much deeper and expands the comparison into places where our subconscious minds take over and reveal layers we never knew were there.

When we convert our character into a setting, we start to think about this person in ways we rarely, if ever, see the people in our lives, or in our stories. The smallest details become important, sometimes even critical, to the fullness of the setting. These details then translate into a fuller, more realistic character. Specific types of clothing or colors, the order or disorder of the character's personality, can become hallmarks of the setting. Secrets the character has kept from us can leap to the fore and help send us in directions we hadn't thought of but that enhance our story a hundred-fold.

An added advantage is that by converting the character to a setting, we can discover metaphors that we can then use throughout the story to reveal the character on a deeper level—metaphors we might not know about otherwise. For instance, I discovered a lichen-slicked rock in the corner of one *Character As Setting* exercise, where moisture dripped with unrelenting regularity. It was a detail that surprised me as I crafted this character into a setting, for I hadn't thought of him as that dangerous even though he was the greedy, unscrupulous antagonist. Now whenever that character appears water drips somewhere and the scene is dark and gritty, usually in a cavern, on a rock-strewn shore, or in the depths of the stone castle.

It's not a metaphor I would have thought of on a conscious level, but it has helped shape this character into a deep, dark, threatening force of nature. The dark stone and dripping water have become an evil omen of danger-to-come that the reader recognizes well before the protagonists do. This metaphor has helped build the story into layers that have brought out hidden strengths and talents in my protagonists, and taken the plot in directions that have made it even more exciting. The enhanced struggles pull readers deep into the story. They can't stop turning pages. And isn't that what we, as writers, want?

*Exercise #9: Character as Setting**

(Purpose of Exercise: To find greater depths in the character through a shift in view)

TAKE THE CHARACTER YOU have been working with, or another major character from your story, and turn that character into a setting. Ask yourself: What kind of setting would this person be, if he or she were a place instead of a person? What aspects of that person would make this setting unique and memorable to the reader? Write a detailed description of the setting. This is **not a scene**; there are **no characters.** It is a **detailed description only** of the setting itself.

Try to define your character's personality as particular aspects of the setting. This is not a place in which you would find the character living (like the *Private Spaces* exercise above), but a character actually turned into one of the settings for the story. This does not necessarily mean you would use this setting in your story, although if it works by all means incorporate it into the writing. This is simply another, unique way to view who your character truly is.

The purpose of this exercise is to get you thinking about your character in broader and deeper terms than if you consider the character as merely a living, breathing human being (or animal or otherworldly creature, if that is the case). It's also, as I've said, a great way to discover objects to use as metaphors that you can add to story settings to reflect and enhance certain aspects of your characters' personalities, and multi-layer the story.

As you create your character as a setting, consider how the place would smell, the sounds you might hear, the atmosphere that pervades the area, the lighting and the textures, as well as the things you would find there. Consider carefully how each aspect of your character's personality would translate into both place and objects as you write a detailed description of the character as a setting.

Now set your timer for **15 MINUTES** and start writing. When you finish, you might want to repeat this exercise with all your major characters.

Examples From My Class Writing

WHEN I TEACH MY "What If" Writing Group classes, I don't just stand at the front of the room and instruct. I also participate, doing each of the exercises with my students. I do this for a number of reasons, not the least of which is that I, too, still have much to learn about writing. But I also do it to help my students understand and analyze their own work by giving them something written by a published author/professional editor against which to compare it.

This is not to say that what I write is always perfect; there are times when it falls short of the mark, when I could have done much better. Still, I thought that some of you might want a little of what I produce in the classes as clarifying examples in case of confusion, or to use as a yardstick against which to measure your understanding of the lessons, since we're not able to share face-to-face. Just be aware that of what follows, nothing is edited, tweaked or polished. Everything is a product of timed writing sessions done during my actual classes.

Lesson #1: Create a Character

Character's Age: 31

Eye Color: Green with blue flecks

Hair Color: Red, carroty red, brash and vibrant

Name of City/Town: Gradyville

Type of Place: Small Town

Type of Residence: cheap single mobile home on outskirts of town

Character's Name: Graciela Farok

Prominent facial feature: buck teeth

Passion: Collecting dragonflies

Quirk: sucks on hair when nervous

Gender: Woman

Nothing ever worked out the way I hoped it would when Big Sal—Daddy—finally returned home. We thought life would get better. Why I don't know. After all he'd just finished a ten-to-twenty stretch at Mason Correctional for aggravated assault. He'd actually tried to kill Buddy, but he was never very good with his fists. He shoulda known better and took the Smith & Wesson with him. But that was Daddy, always thinking after the fact.

Cherry was running pretty wild in those days. She was my younger sister, only fourteen at the time. Still could be—my sister, I mean, not fourteen—but I don't know where she is now. Could be dead for all I know. Or care.

But anyway, Cherry just jumped on Big Sal's back, minute he waltzed through the door. And by waltz, I mean he kicked it open stead of trying the knob. Still dented in the shape of his foot, which lets you know how my life's turned out. Anyway, Cherry, she was all over him. Ma had walked out a couple years before, run off with Buddy when she realized Big Sal would get out eventually, so it was just me and Cherry. And Griff, the baby.

I loved that boy, I did. He was bout twelve years younger than me and I pretty much raised him from the time he was born. More my kid than Ma's or Sal's. He was nine the year Sal come back, and a good kid. Made his bed, did his chores, paid attention in school even if reading was hard for him. And polite. Said, "Yes'm" and "No'm" like clockwork and even "Sorry" when need be. And meant it, too.

Things was pretty good til Sal kicked his way back into the family. I was working at the diner then, waiting tables and fending off the jerks that make up the male population of this crappy berg. Cherry was being fourteen, teasing everything in pants and thinking she'd keep getting away with it. And Griff? Well, Griff was Griff, just coasting along day by day, doing whatever he could to stay out of trouble.

Sal took one look at him—Cherry still hanging on his neck—and knew Griff warn't his. I could see it in his eyes, the knowledge that hit him like a two-by-four. I tried to stop him. But he was so strong—all that weight lifting in the joint—and then little Griff was just lying there, not moving. And Cherry was screaming fit to beat the band, so Sal haul's off and slugs her, too. Seems jail ain't no good for learning how to deal with a temper.

Lesson #3: Who Are They?

Skylark is the kind of person who cannot abide a puzzle or an unanswered question. She has a driving need to know the answers, to solve the problems, not because it will help the people involved (or so she believes) but because she only knows who she is in relation to the world when all is in order. When she is in control. That is why she has become a private investigator.

She allows herself to feel little affection for or connection to other people, preferring to work solo and answer only to herself. She buries her feelings deep beneath her rather hard-boiled surface, an image she has worked hard to cultivate. However, her deep-seated need for contact and connection, a need she buries from her own awareness, shows in the form of a love of literature. She is an avid reader of philosophical fiction and alternative fiction, as well as character-driven mystery and suspense.

Her client reports tend to be clinical and fact-based, with little or no digression into the whys and wherefores of the situations. She rarely allows herself to contemplate or talk about her past, choosing to believe it is over and done with. She rarely lets anyone get close to her and is usually proven right in her assumption that most people are users, since she subconsciously gravitates toward those who will support her belief that trust must be earned and most people aren't worth trust no matter what they do to earn it. She uses every betrayal as another nail in the coffin of her secret emotions. The bane of her existence is her paranormal ability to see the past superimposed over the present. Her biggest fear is that people will find out about that curse. The worst thing that could happen to her is to take on partners. She ends up with three of them, all of whom also have paranormal abilities. And thus is the paranormal detective series born.

Lesson #4: If I Were A...

Character: Diablerie, the amoral Sorceress in Destany's Daughter (Volume 1 of The Unification series), a YA Fantasy in progress.

If Diablerie were a/an:

Animal: madagascar bat, because she intuits the world around her, flies above and beyond everyone, and eats her enemies for sustenance.

Mode of Transportation: a sailing vessel, a Tall Ship, because she sails the seas of necromancy in stealth and complete freedom, reveling in her power and beauty

Dwelling: medieval castle complete with dungeon, because she inspires hopes of greatness, chivalry and heroes arising to overcome.

Garden: a hedge labyrinth made with flowering and poisonous shrubs, because she can be bountiful and gracious, then become cold and calculating in a single turn. Also, the pathway that winds into her core is the same pathway she chose to walk in the opposite direction, away from her core, so now she stands outside herself, unable to look in and see who she really is.

Vegetable: Artichoke, because she has so many hidden places inside her, and so much armor protecting her heart.

Weather Pattern: A snowstorm in Alaska because her inability to understand her own feelings leaves her cold and destructive when she should be warm and compassionate.

TV Program: Who Do You Think You Are? because everything she does is merely a way for her to understand who she is, what her role in life is, and to learn to accept herself as she is.

Article of Clothing: a long, hooded velvet cape, because she is capable of protecting those she feels deserve her protection, and because she can hide within it.

Type of Footwear: High black leather boots with steel toes and 3" heels, because she trods on those weaker than she is and kicks those who don't agree with her until they do.

Day of the Week: Wednesday, because Wednesday is the pivotal day of the week, exactly in the center, the turning point as it were. Wednesday is everything Diablerie fears: it's the median, its potential apt to be overlooked.

Type of Music: a great classical symphony because it's majestic and full of longing, and filled with subtle nuances only the adept can differentiate.

Piece of Furniture: A daybed, because she is changeable, able to be what she needs to be when the situation calls for it.

Geographical Formation: A caldera, because though quiet, there is potential for great destruction that will change the landscape of the future, and change the destiny of all who dwell nearby. Wisps of smoke, underlying rumbles and emanations of heat give clues to the mysteries that lie deep within.

Lesson #6: Characters and Their Desires: Dilemma Choices

Character: Skylark, A Psychic P. I. (from my upcoming psychic detective series set in Los Osos, CA)

A) If Skylark were given a bonus or promotion for a project she didn't complete on her own, she would make sure the "powers that be" understood fully that she did not work alone and would accept no thanks or remuneration of any kind unless each person who worked on the project was included. However, she would also want any bonus prorated according to how much each person did. Fairness is of paramount importance to her, since she never felt she was treated fairly when she was growing up.

B) If Skylark got home from shopping and found a whole bag of expensive meats in her possession that she hadn't paid for, she would call the store first before returning the items. She'd want to know what they would do with the stuff before turning it over to them. If they hadn't heard from the person who it belongs to, or would throw the meat out (which according to law they would have to, since it had been out of the store's possession), Skylark would donate the meat to a homeless shelter kitchen if she couldn't get it back to the rightful owner.

C) If Skylark found a wallet she would return it intact. No questions asked. And she wouldn't accept a "reward" for doing the right thing. When it's right, it's right. You just do it. Period. Only a turd would ask for a reward for doing what she should have done in the first place.

Lesson #7: What's In A Name?

Names of Characters:

1) White-Collar Thief: Stanley Wycoff

2) Bitter woman: Gertrude Unterfelt

3) Shy Young Man: Joseph Malloy

4) Womanizer: Cyrano Lovelace

5) Grandmother: Ima Richman (Sherilee Mathers)

6) Fearful Bank Teller: Conrad (aka Connie) Johnson

7) Brave HS Principal: Benton Steele

8) Class Bully: Jack Macomber

9) Class Clown: Willy Willis

10) Joking Checkout Clerk: Harvey Lipschitz

11) Anal Cop: Dirk Dickerson

12) Accountant: Hunter Powers

13) Small Town Pastor: Paul Polenski

14) Large City Pastor: Simon Masterson

15) Honest Politician: Truman Roberts

16) Legal Aid Attorney: Collin Montgomery

17) Criminal Defense Attorney: Stansfield Turner

18) Secret Arsonist/Firefighter: Aaron Lightfinger

19) English Prof: Cecily Rhodes

20) Used Car Salesman: August Spencer

21) My Character: Skylark—will not change because it reflects what she sees as her heritage. Having one name makes her stand out in a crowd, which she likes since she felt invisible when growing up. Plus it has a fantasy, imaginative ring to it which reflects her psychic powers.

22)

Lesson #8: Private Spaces

Skylark lives in a small independent structure behind a main house. Might once have been a garage or carriage house converted to living quarters.

My first impression of this place is one of economy. Everything is white or ecru: the carpet, the walls, the upholstery, even the vase on the coffee table is white. There are few decorations: two paintings on the wall of abstract design in which blue and purple predominate; yellow daisies in the white vase; copper cookware hanging from a ceiling rack in the kitchen partition; a blue and violet plaid chenille throw over the back of the sofa.

It's a spacious-feeling room even with its small size, probably because everything is well-proportioned for the space, and the compulsive neatness lends an air of peace and tranquility. I can see a few photographs on the night stand and the eating bar, the silver filigree of the frames an odd note of Victorian overindulgence amidst the soothing calm of the white. The photos show small groupings of women at various functions, the vibrant colors of their fancy dress sounding like cymbals in the room.

An area rug lies atop the white carpet beneath the mahogany coffee table, its pattern of scattered brown and gold leaves on an ecru ground merely an echo of the various furnishings. I don't see a bed and assume the sofa pulls out. The only truly incongruous notes, aside from the picture frames, is the ancient roll-top desk in the corner. I can see papers sticking out from beneath the roll-top, and scattered across the top of the desk is a handful of change, a pair of black leather gloves, a black lace scarf, a hair clip and three dog biscuits. There is no other hint of a canine, or any pet, in the entire place.

The other odd note is the oak bookcase, filled with classics, philosophy, mysteries and police and forensics manuals. The person who lives here is very reserved, even with herself. She doesn't dwell on sentiment and prefers her environment to be calm and under control. But there are depths lying unplumbed, depths that either she is not aware of or, more likely, that she doesn't want people to know about.

She has an adventurous spirit that she keeps on a tight leash, though it breaks out every once in a while, gets away from her until she has to close it back within the roll-top desk. She probably has a solitary job, one that allows her the freedom to make her own hours and rules, and not have to be at someone else's beck and call. I doubt she is a police officer because of the rules. If she is in law enforcement, she is probably a private cop or investigator. She keeps herself to herself and doesn't let anyone in, often not even herself. She is as much an enigma to herself as she is to others.

Lesson #9: Character as Setting

Character: Skylark, Private Detective, who was abandoned at birth

The stable sat off by itself as though in self-imposed isolation, a building half-regal in its graceful symmetrical lines, half-commoner with its shabby flaking paint and windows twisted awry in their frames. It gave the impression that it was uncomfortable in its own skin, built for a purpose it was still unsure of even after years of fulfilling its destiny.

The main double doors had stuck ajar, so to enter you had to inch sideways through the gap into dusty dimness little relieved by the narrow windows near the peaked roof. Sturdy beams criss-crossing overhead lent a feel of confidence, as though the edifice could withstand years of abuse unscathed. The comforting aroma of hay drifted on the warm air currents and crackled underfoot. Hay bales set around the walls invited visitors to sit and relax, to let the building take control for a while.

Reality took on a deeper dimension within the structure. Time slowed to a crawl or moved forward in quantum leaps. The well of possibilities stood in the center of the huge room, bucket and ladle hanging ready for visitors to sample a few of the myriad alternate events of life lived on the in-between planes.

Horses of many types and colors filled the numerous stalls, their restless movements and huffing breaths a tense counterpoint to the relaxed atmosphere. Pigeons flew overhead in the lofts, darting through the half-open windows, stitching together the otherworldly dreams of the interior with the harsh fabric of everyday reality outside the barn. Tension filled the air as hooves dug runnels in the soft wood of the plank floor. One had the feeling that at any moment a horse would bolt from its stall, thunder through the gap in the doors, and range free in the outside world in order to bring ordered meaning to unknown chaos.

Contrasting with the rough, unfinished wood of the walls and floor, expensive tack lined one side of the barn: saddles of suede-soft leather; bits of sterling silver; reins and halters of braided cashmere. Central in the display was a blank space, something missing. A puzzle piece lost long ago, without which the mosaic of life and time would never be complete. It was a place that invited and rejected simultaneously, that embraced the cultured with the crass in a space of vulnerability as fragile as a crazed glass vase.

Unit 2: Setting

"Don't tell me the moon is shining; show me the glint of light on broken glass."
~Anton Chekhov

SETTING INCLUDES ALL THE places where a story takes place. These locations can be physical, and they can also be mental. Stephen King is master of the psychological setting, which he used with immense success in such stories as *Misery* and *The Shining*.

Settings help ground your story in reality, even if that reality is the fantastical world of science fiction or fantasy. Settings give readers a frame of reference that can serve as a metaphor for the theme of the story, reflect the growth and changes the main characters undergo, and help readers understand the connections between characters and their desires. Setting is also the landscape of the entire world where the story takes place. Landscape is more than the sum of its individual places; it's the entire atmosphere—the sights, sounds, smells and textures that create the world in which your characters live and breathe.

By creating a realistic world in which your characters can work to achieve their needs, you make the entire milieu of the story come alive. What follows are **7 in-depth exercises** on creating fascinating settings your readers will not forget.

Unit 2, Setting: Contents

Lesson #1: Creating A Setting

A SETTING IS MORE than simply the location where events take place. The setting serves to ground readers in the story, and gives them a frame of reference from which to understand the actions and motivations of the characters. If the setting is nonexistent, or not fully enough rendered, the characters and the action will feel as though they are floating in a vacuum. Nothing makes sense, and when things don't make sense to readers they put down the story, or close the book.

It's not enough to merely state that the characters are sitting at a table in a bakery. To be fully engaged in the scene, readers will also need to know other important information, some of which, for example, might be what kind of bakery it is, where in the city or town it is located, how well it is kept up, what is baked there, what the characters have ordered to eat and drink, what other kinds of customers are there with them, what scents predominate, what the weather outside is like, etc. **The reality of a setting lies in its details**. A master writer can paint a vivid picture that will enthrall readers.

Through judicious selection of details, the writer can create a homey atmosphere, or an aura of love and happiness. Or an atmosphere of menace. Maybe a pall of despair, or a stark realism that makes readers hold their breath. Or perhaps just a feel of uneasiness in the air, a building tension that keeps the reader turning pages. Simple things, like what the characters order and how they eat it (or not, as the case may be), can reveal hidden aspects of the characters' personalities or give clues to their motivations. What the point of view character chooses to reveal about the setting can often reveal as much or even more about him- or herself as it does about the setting.

Beyond that, vivid descriptions of the setting scattered throughout the scene keeps readers grounded in the scene. The setting serves as a reminder to readers of where the characters are as the story continues to unfold. Movies and television do it with what they call "establishing shots"—those short clips of the boat-laden waterfront ("CSI: Miami"), the scientific lab ("Bones") or swaying palm trees and grass skirts ("Hawaii 5-O") that lead into the action. Writers need to incorporate their own version of the "establishing shot" into their scenes to keep readers from forgetting where the story is taking place.

We've all read stories where the scenes were either not adequately described, or not referred to often enough. After a while we start to wonder, "Are they still in the cave, or are they back at the hotel?" And we start to flip back, scanning here and there to find out. Which takes us out of the story and drains away our enjoyment of the plot. It splits our focus and makes us less likely to return to the story, more likely to put the book down. And maybe not pick it up again. What writers want are readers who are so fully engaged that they cannot tear themselves away from the story. They keep turning those pages, far into the night. Vivid, compelling settings will help us achieve just that.

READ: *The Novel Writer's Toolkit* (Mayer, 2003), Page 128, Setting, to the end of the first paragraph on page 129.

*Exercise #1: Creating A Setting**

(Purpose of exercise: To learn to consider all aspects of a setting, not just physical description.)

PICK ONE OF THE following places and make it a setting for your story. Describe the setting in detail, remembering to add such items as sounds and smells and the way things feel as well as how they look. Concentrate on bringing the setting alive by adding information on the people who are there, the weather, the socioeconomic structure, the seasons, the architecture, the physical terrain. Your character can be alone, or interact with another character. You can have dialogue or not. But remember, interaction between characters, if any, should be kept to a minimum. The main aim here is to **describe this setting as fully as possible**.

Now choose a setting, set your timer for **15 MINUTES** and start writing.

1. A city park
2. A church building
3. A cemetery
4. The waterfront
5. An airport
6. A restaurant
7. A forest clearing
8. A train or bus station
9. An office
10. A school building or campus

Lesson #2: Setting, Symbol and Theme

SYMBOLS ARE VERY POWERFUL in our culture. In a story, the repetition of a symbol acts on the subconscious mind allowing us to recognize, if only on a subconscious level, the clues that are dropped along the way as the plot unfolds. Symbols stand as easily recognizable and understood metaphors for the larger-than-life themes of our lives as reflected in the stories we tell. They tell us to "pay attention, this is important!" whenever they appear.

Consider the movie *The Sixth Sense*. The color red is used as a symbol throughout the movie, a signal to the viewer that whenever the main character appears, something is different. Something has changed. Something is wrong. Pay attention. Not until the end (spoiler alert!) do we consciously realize that he is dead, and has been from before the movie began. But shocking as it is, we do not react in anger or feel manipulated or cheated by the writers. When the revelation unfolds, our subconscious, which has picked up on the symbol scattered throughout the movie, says, amidst our surprise, "So *that's* what it is. I knew something wasn't quite right. Now I understand."

Symbols have the power to touch us very deeply. Wise writers who can weave symbolism into their stories achieve a fascinating depth that keep readers enthralled with the story, even if on a subconscious level. It's what makes readers say, "I don't quite know what's going on yet, but I just can't put the book down. I have to find out."

Symbols can be things, actions or a character's belief. When we find an authentic symbol that is generic to the story—whatever form it takes—it will work to add meaning and depth to the story. One great place to find symbols is in our settings. They are rife with objects, animals, scents, sounds, textures, etc, that can stand for the characters' deepest selves. When we add these kinds of layers to our stories, we add tension and interest, two of the main qualities that keep readers reading.

READ: *The Novel Writer's Toolkit* (Mayer, 2003) Page 129, Symbolism

Exercise #2: Setting, Symbol and Theme*

(Purpose of exercise: To learn to use the setting to enhance and deepen the story's theme.)

USE THE SETTING YOU created for the last exercise. Examine the details you find in that setting and consider whether each one could be used symbolically in your story. Then list each detail that could be a possible symbol, and explain how that symbol might function in the story, what the symbolism could be and how it would affect the characters or action as the story unfolds. (For example, in the bakery setting noted above, the smell of lemon pie could be a symbol of the protagonist's subconscious need to recreate the childhood home she lost when she was twelve. Every time she smells lemons, she goes home determined to incorporate something from her past into her present life, regardless of what the other people in her family want, even though she does not realize the scent of lemon is what triggers that determination.)

Set your timer for **20 MINUTES** and write until the buzzer goes off.

Lesson #3: Unexpected Setting Details

WRITE WHAT YOU KNOW. We've probably all been given (or will be given) that piece of advice somewhere along the way in our writing career. But if writers heeded that advice to the letter, there would be no such genres as science fiction, fantasy, historical fiction or even mystery and suspense. After all, not many of us are willing to commit murder just to write about it. And traveling to another galaxy or dimension just isn't within the scope of modern technology at this point.

And there's no need. Writers, thankfully, write from very vivid imaginations. But just as readers need a foundation, so do writers. We need a way to keep our imaginations grounded so that we, and our readers, can understand what we imagine and image it along with us. We need to be able to frame it in terms both we and our readers can comprehend.

The same applies to our settings. Yes, as Elizabeth George writes, it's best if we can actually visit Paris if we want to set a story there. It would be easier to describe the rocks, the cold, the thin air and biting snow of the Matterhorn had we actually scaled it ourselves. And it would be a (relative) snap to recreate the hurricane that flooded New Orleans had we lived through Katrina in person.

But we can't always go to the places where we want to set our stories, not in person, anyway. But we can visit most locations through movies, other books and the internet. And we can tap into our own life experiences to fill in any gaps.

For example, we cannot hop a rocket and colonize a new planet, but we probably do know what it feels like to move to a new area (or even just a new school) where we felt alienated, where we didn't know where anything was or how to act at certain times. We may not have actually killed anyone, but we probably know how it feels to be angry enough to want to. We might not have lost a child or a mate, but we probably do remember how we felt when a beloved pet died, or our best friend moved away. And so, by tapping into our own emotions, we can write believable stories about colonizing Ordeva, plotting the death of Mr. McNab, or a mother rebuilding her life after her son dies of cancer.

We have, stored within us, a lifetime's worth of experiences that have evoked emotions similar to those we need to develop for our stories. And we can tap into those experiences and emotions to bring the correct atmosphere to the settings we create. Atmosphere is, after all, simply emotion floating in the air. You may at times even find unexpected details popping up in your settings, things you hadn't consciously considered but that your subconscious knew you needed. That is merely your subconscious trawling the sea of your life experience for verisimilitude.

Learning to tap into our past experiences is not always easy. It takes courage and fortitude. Some emotions are difficult to revisit and deal with. But doing so allows us to bring true richness to our settings. It lends authenticity to our rendering of each place, because **the emotions evoked are authentic** to our lives. And, at times, we might find our plots deepening or a subplot opening up in ways we hadn't before considered.

READ: *Write Away* (George, 2004) Page 24, starting at the 2nd full paragraph from the bottom, to page 25, ending after the first sentence in the second full paragraph.

Exercise #3: Incorporating Unexpected Details*

(Purpose of Exercise: To learn to incorporate the unexpected into our settings.)

AS FAST AS YOU can, write down the first answer you think of to the following items. Don't stop to think, just write as fast as you can. Go!

1. A place
2. A color
3. A sound
4. A smell
5. An emotion
6. A texture
7. A weather phenomenon
8. A favorite food
9. A hated article of clothing
10. A pet of some kind

Now, set the timer for **20 MINUTES.** Become one of the characters in your story. Take your list of answers and, **as that character,** write about the setting in which you find yourself. Don't stop to think, just write whatever comes to mind—**as that character.** Make sure you **use all ten answers** in your writing. It doesn't matter whether you think these answers fit the character or not. Allow your subconscious figure out a way to use them believably as you write.

The purpose of this exercise is to show you how to adapt the details that need to be in your story to the events and the characters that populate the story. This will help you accommodate unexpected details that: 1) can arise as your writing progresses and your characters continue to reveal themselves to you; and/or 2) come from your own experience of life and are not therefore necessarily authentic to the chosen setting, but are needed for the purposes of the story.

What you write here can be part of your story, or can be part of the backstory or a scene that happens outside the story—or even after the story has ended. Just trust your instincts and **keep writing for 20 minutes** as you weave these details into your scene.

Lesson #4: Setting As Character

A CHARACTER'S PRIVATE SPACE, or individual setting, can reveal an immense amount of information about the character. And rendering the character as a setting helps us see the character in a different light and discover aspects of his or her personality we might not have noticed before. (See also **Unit #1, Character: Lessons #7 and #8**)

Reversing that process can reveal an immense amount about a setting, and how that setting can be integrated into the totality of the story instead of merely being a background locale against which the drama (or comedy) unfolds. Why? Because it's easier for us to understand people, to see nuances in humans that we often miss in the environment. This is because people are endlessly fascinating to us. They are capricious. Mystifying. Ever-changing. Even people we know well can often surprise us.

But our environment pretty much stays the same, barring natural disaster or man-made catastrophe. We don't consciously notice the trees and bushes, the birds and squirrels, the signs along the roadways, the sidewalks (or lack of them), or the stores that line the street. Even the sky is pretty much "invisible" most of the time. These things are the same, day after day, month after month. They become the background landmarks that we take for granted and stop seeing after a while. That's why, if the willow grove on the corner is cut down, we find ourselves getting lost in familiar territory. Or why we're shocked and surprised when we go into the new store we noticed just two days ago and find out it's been open for over six months, nine month, even a year or more. We don't notice what doesn't affect us until it does.

A great way to become fully aware of the settings we use in our stories is to turn them into characters. By making the inanimate animate, we imbue them with irresistible interest. We open our eyes and really look at them. We can delve into their psyches to see what makes them "tick." We find nuances we hadn't known were there. We're faced with surprises that can make our story more vivid and enticing to readers.

Best of all, when we return our "Setting Character" to its natural state, the locale of the story, we often find it has an influence on the human characters, and on the flow of the plot, that it didn't have before. In other words, the setting becomes an intrinsic and inextricable part of the story, a character in its own right. Which just makes our story better.

READ: *Write Away* (George, 2004), Page 19, starting with second full paragraph, to page 24, ending after third full paragraph from the bottom.

*Exercise #4: Setting as Character**

(Purpose of Exercise: To consider setting as a character in your story.)

TAKE THE SETTING YOU have been working with, or another major setting from your story, and turn that setting into a character. Ask yourself: What kind of person would this setting be, if it were human instead of a place? What aspects of the setting would make this person unique and memorable to the reader? Write a detailed description of this person. Remember, this is not a scene, it is **a descriptive biography** of a person.

Try to define specific aspects of the setting as parts of the character's personality. Is this a happy person, or sad? Angry or indifferent? Is it a woman or a man—or a child? Is this person a loner or a joiner? What does he/she look like? Favorite color, food, movie, book? Does this character have siblings, a family, a job, a hobby? Is he/she law abiding or a criminal? Be as detailed as you can be as you weave the elements of this place into human form.

The purpose of this exercise is to get you thinking about your setting in broader and deeper terms than if you consider it merely the backdrop for the story. It's also a great way to discover things you can add to story settings that make them truly memorable to readers, and that help to shape the people and events that happen in the story.

As you create your setting as a person, consider how the character would smell, the sound of the character's voice, his or her moral compass, upbringing, religious beliefs, social acuity, needs and desires. What does this person think about the other characters in the story?
Consider carefully how each aspect of the setting would translate into human form as you write this detailed description of your setting as a character.

Now set your timer for **20 MINUTES** and begin turning your setting into a person.

Lesson #5: Setting and the Five Senses

UNLESS WE'RE TRAINED AS method actors, or have a natural inclination for detail, most of us don't notice our environment beyond whether the sun is shining or the snow is shoveled. We think we're observant, but be honest, now—how many of us can close our eyes and describe in excruciating detail what even our own front yard looks like? Do you know how many trees there are? How about in the back yard? How many are visible through the living room windows? And what kind are they? Do they flower? Set fruit? Have seeds or nuts? What color are their leaves? That's easy, green, but—what particular shade(s) of green?

When we think of a place, what most easily comes to mind is what we **see**. When asked to describe a particular place—an office building, for example—most of us will concentrate on what the building looks like: how big it is, what it is constructed of, what color it is, what kind of windows it has, how many stories, doors, and so on. Few of us think in terms of what the building smells like, or sounds like, or even tastes or feels like.

And yet, life is lived in all 5 sense dimensions: **sight, sound, touch, taste,** and **smell**. Wherever we are, wherever we go, we are bombarded with sensory impressions on all 5 levels. We discover our surroundings through all these sense portals, and make sense of the world by using the information they bring us. In fact, the two most important senses, those that most strongly evoke memory and emotion, are scent and taste. And yet, these are rarely used in setting descriptions.

Therefore, if we are to render fully realized settings for our readers, we must incorporate **the same kind of sensory detail** into the places where we set our stories as we encounter in everyday life. Our settings need to be as complete and realistic as possible, and so we cannot rely on one sense alone to convey the true feel of the place. We must learn to be aware of even the arcane details of place.

READ: *The 38 Most Common Fiction Writing Mistakes* (Bickham, 1992), Pages 58-60 ("Don't Ever Stop Observing and Making Notes")

Exercise #5: Using All Five Senses in a Setting

(Purpose of Exercise: To learn to use all 5 senses to render a fully realized setting.)

THIS EXERCISE COMES IN 6 parts. Make sure you understand each part before you begin. Give yourself **10 MINUTES EACH** for **Parts 1 - 4,** and **15 MINUTES** for **Part 5.**

PART 1) Pick one of the places below and write a **short scene** in which the setting is described in terms of <u>sound</u> only. Do not describe the way it looks, tastes, smells or feels, only the way it sounds. Do **not** state specifically where or what the place is. Let the reader infer the what and/ or where from your description alone. Since this is a scene (though a **short** one), you can have up to two characters in it, but keep dialogue and inner thought to a minimum. Concentrate on creating a full, believable setting your reader can clearly imagine using <u>sound only</u>. Set your timer for **10 MINUTES** and start to write.

A) A Church or Synagogue
B) A Bakery
C) A Steel Mill
D) A Park in the middle of a city
E) A Zoo or Animal Preserve
F) A Laboratory

PART 2) Now rewrite the same scene, describing it in terms of <u>scent only</u>, again not telling what/where but only using smells to make the setting come alive. What changes do you have to make to accommodate scent instead of sound? Give yourself **10 MINUTES** for this.

PART 3) Once again, rewrite your scene, concentrating this time on <u>textures</u> and how things feel to the touch. What needs to be altered when focusing only on the sense of feel? Set the timer for **10 MINUTES**.

PART 4) The fourth rewrite of the scene will focus on **sight**, on only what you can see in this unnamed place. You will once again need to alter things in order to concentrate on the sense of sight. Give yourself **10 MINUTES** to do this part.

PART 5) The fifth rewrite uses only those things you can **taste** to describe the place. You will need to be very creative in your use of taste in this version of the scene description. Think of the many ways one can taste things and use that in your rendering of the scene as you write for **10 MINUTES**.

PART 6) Now, **combine elements from all four versions** of this scene into one fully-textured scene that evokes **all the senses**. Again, don't say specifically where/what the place is. As you write, consider which sensory input is most appropriate to each aspect of the setting. Give yourself **15 MINUTES** to write this fully-sensated scene.

When you have finished this exercise, take a moment to analyze the process. Ask yourself: Which sense do you find most easy to work with? Which one is the most difficult for you to remember to include, and what can you do to remind yourself to use that sense? How much deeper and more real do you think your setting is in this scene when you include as many senses as you can? What can you do to remind yourself to use all five senses when creating your scenes?

Lesson #6: Handling Description

THERE ARE FIVE DIFFERENT ways to deliver information (i.e., tell your story) to readers, and each has its own speed within the confines of the story, from very slow to rapid. They are:

1. Exposition
2. Description
3. Narrative
4. Dialogue
5. Narrative Summary

Exposition is the slowest way to deliver information because **nothing is happening**. It's all just data: biographical, forensic, social, etc. There's no story movement whatsoever.

Next comes **Description**, which are **word pictures of characters and settings**. Because skilled writers can evoke atmosphere and emotion when describing settings, the pace of description is a little faster than mere exposition, though it's still very slow. (The faster delivery systems —Narrative, Dialogue and Narrative Summary—will be detailed in *Unit 6: Dialogue* and *Unit 7: Scenes*.)

However, too much description at the wrong time can bring your tale to a screeching halt. Imagine a suspense-filled scene where, in the dark of a moonless midnight, the hero must save the heroine who is lashed to the railroad tracks with a speeding train approaching. He must fight through a field of thorny bushes and evade the booby traps the villain has set for him and still reach the tracks in time to free his love.

Now imagine that the writer deviates from the tense action to spend three pages describing the environment: the rolling landscape, the types of bushes, the length of the thorns, the shapes and colors of the leaves, the clouds obscuring the half moon and stars, the shadows of surrounding trees, the sound and feel of the capricious wind, the scents blown into the field from nearby restaurants, the shape of the booby traps and what lies within them, the gleam of the tracks, the weathering of the ties, the kind of cinders and gravel between the rails, the sound of the approaching train... by now our eyes are crossing and we're skipping whole paragraphs trying to get back to the action.

There are **two important things** to remember when rendering a description, whether it be of the settings or the characters. First, **weave the details into the action as it occurs**; and second, **only give readers what they need to know at that moment** to understand and picture the story in their minds.

This requires two skills on the part of the writer. First, we must learn how to pick the details that best render the setting, not just the obvious ones. And second, we must learn when to give our readers the information they need to visualize the scene at that moment—and nothing more.

Often this means we will overwrite the setting at first, which is good because it gives us enough detail for the second step, which is to later analyze those details and refine them (i.e., cut swaths through them) so that we paint a clear picture as economically as possible. We must ask ourselves all along the way: Does the reader **need** to have all these details to visualize the setting? And does the reader need to have all this information **right now**, or can some of it be inserted later?

As you complete Exercise #6, keep in mind the previous lesson. Sight is not the only way to describe a setting, and sometimes it's not even the best way. Evoking scents, sounds, tastes and/or textures in just a sentence or two might open whole vistas of imaginative visualization for the reader that three or four paragraphs of sight description will not.

<u>READ:</u> *The 38 Most Common Fiction Writing Mistakes* (Bickham), Page 14-16 ("Don't Describe Sunsets")

Exercise #6: Handling Description

(Purpose of Exercise: To learn to render an easily-visualized setting within the context of the story's action.)

CHOOSE ONE OF THE following scenarios and write a scene between two characters. They do not both have to be protagonists; one can be the hero/heroine and one the villain (protagonist and antagonist), if you choose. In the scene, one character must strive to save the other from danger or disaster, whether the other character wants saving or not.

Write this scene as if it is new to the story. The reader has not yet been exposed to this particular location, so you must render the setting as fully as possible while keeping the taut action moving forward. Now choose your setting scenario, set your timer for **15 MINUTES** and write.

A. On a mountain climbing trip, one character looses his/her grip and hangs from a fast-fraying rope.

B. The dam has burst and water has filled the house almost to the rooftop. The foundations are threatening to collapse and cast one character into the raging waters.

C. A bank robbery has locked one character in the airtight vault, and the air is running out.

D. The car has stalled on the railroad tracks with a train approaching. One character is trapped inside the vehicle with jammed door locks and seat belt.

E. One character is trapped on a ship run aground on a reef. A wild gale threatens to tear it apart and keeps rescue boats from approaching.

F. Deep in a jungle, one character has stepped on the trigger switch for a bomb. Venomous snakes, man-eating animals and man-made booby traps surround the scene.

Lesson #7: Setting and Landscape

NOW WE COME TO the landscape of our story. Landscape is **not** the same as the setting or settings, although we may find writers who use the words interchangeably. They are **not interchangeable**. Settings are the individual places where the action of the story takes place. The landscape of the story is larger than that, for it encompasses the emotion and aura of the entire milieu.

The landscape has to **evoke a visceral response** within readers that connects them to the story. Without this emotional connection, readers have no reason to continue reading. It is this emotional connection that compels the reader to care about the characters and about the outcome of the story. Without that connection, all the writer has is merely a closed book no one particularly wants to open. When a place becomes real to the reader, it produces an emotional connection the reader cannot ignore.

The landscape is all-inclusive and is particular to the locale and time wherein the story occurs. It's more than a description of what a place looks like, it's what makes the place unique and unforgettable. It includes all the intangibles that make a place truly memorable, the atmospheric framework that contains and colors the story. (Check out the

Alaskan mysteries of Sue Henry and Dana Stabenow for unforgettable landscape rendering.) Whether you have one limited area where your story takes place, or multiple settings, you must frame it all in one believable landscape.

Think about a place you visited and still remember, years later. What about it made it so unforgettable? It wasn't just the way the buildings looked, or the trees, or the mountains. If you stop to really think about it, you will remember the way the air felt as it brushed against your skin, the scents that rode the air currents, the feel of the sun on your face, the color and depth of the sky, the way the people moved and interacted, what they wore, their vehicles, the animals and the wildlife, what plants, flowers and trees grew there, how things felt to the touch. Plus all the things you may have expected, but were missing.

Time also affects landscapes. The Chicago of 1930 is not the same Chicago of 2012. People do not do the same things, or do them in the same way. Buildings have their own sounds and smells in each era. The weather exerts different kinds of influences on the city. When using historical settings for our stories, or settings that take place on other worlds or in other universes, we must keep in mind the way time and distance can change the very atmosphere of a place.

As writers, when we travel we need to notice these kinds of details. It's always a good idea to carry a writer's notebook to jot down both obvious and intangible details about different places. Then we can go back and analyze what makes the sky different in Denver than in New York City, and different again from that which cups the Kansas prairie. Or why the sounds of the birds in the Adirondaks are not the same as those of the Rockies, and the gull cries of the East Coast are not the same as those of West Coast gulls. The light of sunset paints a completely different picture in Miami than it does in Big Sur. The rustle of palm fronds has a distinct sound different from the leaves of maple trees, or quaking aspens, or eucapypti.

All this is part of the story's landscape, the big picture of the total environment of our story. Elizabeth George likens the story landscape to the surface material (canvas, paper, etc.) and paint medium (oils, watercolors, pastels, etc.) the artist uses to render the details of a painting. As the surface and medium change, so does the picture we create and the emotion we evoke in our readers. The details, or the colors we choose to incorporate in the painting, are the setting(s) and characters contained within the surface material and medium of our unique landscape.

Our story landscape must be as real to us as the environment in which we live our daily lives. As writers we must be able to see, touch, taste, smell and hear every nuance of the milieu. Only when it is that real to us will it become real for our readers. Only then will it make a true connection with our readers, which in turn urges them to keep turning pages. When we create a truly authentic landscape, readers will feel they have actually visited it, walked in our characters' footsteps and felt our created sun on their faces, our imagined wind in their hair, and sniffed real smells, with only the magic of our words wafting past their eyes.

READ: *Write Away* (George, 2004), Page 29 to the end of the first paragraph on Page 33

Exercise #7: Defining the Landscape of Your Story*

(Purpose of Exercise: To understand the difference between Setting and Landscape.)

WRITE A DESCRIPTION OF the Landscape of your story, concentrating on those areas that make it unique. Try to address the following points in your Landscape description:

1. How does the story's landscape affect the mood of the story, the scenes, the characters?
2. What happens in the story because of the landscape that wouldn't happen if it were set in another landscape?
3. What would have to change if the story were set in another landscape? How would that affect the story?
4. What effect, if any, does the landscape have on the story arc?
5. How close is your landscape to becoming a character in the story? Or is it more appropriate that your landscape remain in the background?
6. What drew you to this landscape above others?
7. What in your landscape is real and what is made up? How do the made-up elements affect the real ones?
8. Is it easier or harder to work with real elements in the landscape? With the made up elements?
9. In thinking about your story's landscape, do you find there are parts of it you don't know as well as you should? Can you foresee

any possible changes in the story as you explore and get to know the landscape better?

Now, set your timer for **20 MINUTES** and write about your story's landscape, answering the above questions, until the time is up.

Examples From My Class Writing

I'M INCLUDING JUST A few pieces (or partial pieces) I wrote during my *"What If?"* Writing Group classes to help you understand the extent of the lessons in this section. Remember, these are raw pieces as produced in class, without any editing done to them.

Lesson #1: Create a Setting

(I chose #3, The Waterfront, for my setting. Not until the time was up did I realized that the "she" in the scene is psychic detective Skylark, the main character in my paranormal suspense series in progress.)

She noticed the light first, blinding in its intensity as it reflected off the water. It shimmered, that vast expanse of ocean, moving in rhythm to a secret internal clock that echoed the shifts of the universe. Gull caws cracked the brisk air like sharp thunderclaps, or gunshots. The ubiquitous breeze, rushing ashore after its long journey from the Orient, poked and pried into every seam and buttonhole of her clothing, bringing with it the stench of rotting fish, decaying seaweed, spiced with the salt tang of brine. It made her feel alive and dead at the same time, and she relished the conflicting emotions. Fine sand particles stung her face and arms and she shoved her hands into her pockets, seeking both warmth and safety. But there was no safety for her on the dock, or anywhere else for that matter.

Insignificant laughter from yards away danced on the capricious wind, children's innocent voices. The sound grated on her nerves, an irreverent counterpoint to the whoosh of the air, the macabre ululations of the birds. The water slapped the dock, a wet splat that reminded her of the way her foster father's hand had sounded as it hit her flesh. She shuddered. She walked down the dock, her footsteps thudding on the pocked weathered boards, a dull sound of ending. She wondered if the minuscule cracks in the wood would widen as she walked until she slipped through into the icy ocean depths. What scared her most was that no one would ever notice.

Lesson #2: Setting, Symbols and Theme

Possible symbols I found in the above setting, and the two I chose (labeled **Story Symbol**) to be used in my first Skylark paranormal novel:

1. Water - Water as a symbol of life; in the story it's winter, the creek is frozen over, water must be hauled to the house. You have to work at life to live it.

2. Light - illumination, as a symbol of her psychic gifts, her ability to see answers in the darkness; **Story Symbols:** auras that surround her visions; lines of light connecting puzzle pieces of the mystery. These help her understand connections among the puzzle pieces and to solve the mystery.

3. Bird Calls - birds as messengers (Poe's Raven), as a symbol of importance, take heed, be aware. I think in each story it would be a different bird. One that comes and sits on her windowsill, or a tree branch outside the house, or on the fence near where she's standing. It might be the bird call or just the presence that heralds the onset of a vision.

4. Noxious odors spiced with a scent of life (sea brine) — as a symbol of her past rearing its ugly head, and the struggle to live in the darkness of her past; symbol: unpleasant scents that she smells even if no one else can. They distract her attention from the task at hand.

5. The splat of water hitting wood — water sounds as a symbol of both life and pain and fear. Symbol: water dripping. Again, to distract her with visions of the past and not being good enough to do her job.

6. Footsteps thudding — dreams of footsteps thudding, of people walking away from her as a symbol of her struggle to feel she belongs, a symbol of her inability to trust anyone. **Story Symbol:** The sound of footsteps. Heralds the arrival of an antagonist.

Lesson #3: Incorporating Unexpected Details

Words to incorporate: River wharf; Purple; Ringing doorbell; Baking bread; Fear; Rough stucco; Monsoon; Lasagna; Boots; Toucan

Don't ask me how I got here. One minute I was shopping for new shoes and I felt dizzy. I must have passed out; I lost awareness and everything went black—for a moment, an hour, a day, I haven't a clue. Then I woke up. Here. Not that I have any idea where here is, mind you. Parts of it seem familiar—no, everything is familiar taken one-by-one. It's the whole that's out of kilter somehow.

Great predicament for a detective to be in, not knowing where she is. Or when she is. Lot of good my psychic powers will do me now.

It's dark here, black enough that I had to feel my eyes to make sure they were open. Never really appreciated the value of ambient light before. I'd figure I was way out in the country somewhere if the other details—those I can hear, smell and feel—didn't convince me I was still in the middle of a populated area.

I can hear water slapping against wood. The boards beneath me are rough and splintery. They smell of mildew and algae, and in places reek of rotting fish. But the water, for all its restlessness, doesn't have the insatiable rhythm of the ocean. A **river,** maybe? A **dock** jutting out into a swift-flowing current. Definitely far from that wonderful shoe store.

The wind picks up, brings with it the scent of **bread baking**. I swivel my head, trying to get a direction. I don't want to stay on this rickety dock any longer than I have to, but I don't want to risk the proverbial long walk thing. Swimming isn't my strong suit. But the wind keeps changing, shoving at me from one direction, then another, until I'm dizzy with the **fear** of falling into the water. Rain begins to bucket down on me. In seconds I'm drenched, hunched over to take the brunt of the impact on my back. What the hell is going on? Where am I? And why?

I squint between my fingers through the deluge, fighting the **monsoon**-like winds, and off to my left I see a **purple** glow—a light through a translucent curtain? Could shelter be that close? I stumble down the **wharf,** the damned **boots** that I wanted to trade for normal shoes clumping and sliding on the slick wood. I seconds I stumble up against an unseen building, cutting my hands on the rough **stucco**. I feel my way over to the where the purple glow promises a modicum of safety, the baking bread aroma joined now by the luscious richness of **lasagna**. My mouth waters. The purple light emanates from a glass pane in a door. My fingers search. There is no knob. I find a doorbell and push it. Westminster Bells chime somewhere in the depths of the building. A small wizened man in a long robe pulls the door open. A **toucan** perches on his shoulder, gazing at me with unblinking, beady eyes.

"You've come at last," the old man croaks.

And suddenly I am standing blinking in the brightly lit shoe store, dripping monsoon water on the soiled carpet, with yet another psychic mystery to solve.

Lesson #4: Setting as Character

Setting: The shore of a mysterious lake, from *Destany's Daughter*, Volume 1 of The Unification series, a YA Fantasy.

If my setting were a character, she would be a woman of contradictions, capable of lightning-quick changes of mood. She has a restlessness that is integral to her personality, even though there is also a calmness to her, a feeling of patience and acceptance. She lets anyone come within her sphere, though depending on her mood some will have a rough time connecting with her. And yet, even though her passive acceptance draws souls to her, it is her terrible rages that cement the relationship.

She is a tall willowy woman, supple and graceful, but capable of swift, abrupt movements that can spell danger to those close to her. People tend to feel calmed when around her if they are troubled, yet she fills them with a restless feeling, a sense that there is something more, something timeless, that is just out of reach. She is addicting to a great many people.

Her sand colored hair is long, draping past her shoulders in wisps that tend to float on any stray breeze. The bulk of her hair flows down her back almost to her knees. She has an pale oval face with a creamy, rose-and-coral tinged complexion, a small nose, full lips and large pale blue eyes that change to greenish gray when she is angry. Her brows arch up like passive questions that make those around her feel she is interested in them.

She isn't. She wades through life like an independent continent, gathering and losing followers with great unconcern. It is enough for her that there will always be hangers-on who need her. She does not need consistency from them any more than she gives consistency to them. Occasional visits are fine with her and she does not pine away when someone leaves and never returns. Nor does she celebrate those who come to stay.

She wears long flowing robes that sway and dance in the breeze, and goes barefoot most of the time. Her favorite movement is dancing, swooping waltzes that dizzy onlookers and tire out participants. She feels complete in herself and it matters not to her if anyone is harmed or killed when her temper flares. And it does, on a regular though not consistent basis. She is fully as capable of crushing someone as she is of nurturing them, and she has no vested interest in the outcome either way because she knows everyone is replaceable.

She herself does not know where her anger and rage come from. It is part of her makeup and has been since she first became aware of living. It perhaps comes, she thinks, from the selfishness of others, from their inability to comprehend the infinite that surrounds life and from their need to put events into limited personal perspectives. Containment terrifies and enrages her. Because she cannot connect to others, she has no true understanding of limitations. She is as generous in her largesse as she is in her destruction. She is content being who she is and sees no need to ever change, has no desire to connect with or understand others. That is for others to do with her. She is the immovable object and the irresistible force. She is where the stars reach down and touch the earth.

Lesson #7: Landscape

The SomeWhen Murder's landscape consists of an isolated area in southern California through which people pass, but few live in. Those who pass through are on their way to somewhere else, places that have more to offer in terms of civilization, entertainment and employment. Those who live there make their living off those who stop for food, fuel or a night's rest. The community itself is close-knit among themselves, but leery of and aloof with strangers. Their welcome is threaded with distance, and they rarely go the extra mile to help except in the direst circumstances.

Because the story takes place in two time-frames, the landscape changes somewhat. The above paragraph describes modern days. In the past timeframe, the late 1880s, the residents are more welcoming of strangers, although they rarely ask questions of a person's background or reasons for being in Gorman. There is more of a sense of camaraderie among the residents, because new people are settling there still, and there are plans to make it a truly prosperous town and not just a stop-over on the way to somewhere else.

The story takes place in the winter, which affects events because it curtails the residents' abilities to move around in the past time, and because it strands travelers in the present, those who normally would not stop at this place. The open spaces of the past, because the area is not built up, allow the kidnappers to hide the victim from residents who know the area extremely well. And because the community is so close-knit, it makes it more difficult for Skylark to pinpoint the perpetrators.

The landscape is somewhat of a semi-character in that it lends its sense of isolation and space to the story, making events seem either more mysterious or larger than they are. What drew me to this landscape is both its isolation and its position at the top of the Grapevine grade, which ensures that winter conditions would be ripe for forcing Skylark to have to stop there overnight. It's about the only place in So Cal that has that combination of circumstances.

Gorman in the present, which plays little part in the main story, is mostly real; some details of the motor inn and the sometime B&B are made up to fit the needs of the story. Gorman in the past is totally made up; the B&B of the present needed to be in the past, also. I found it easier to make up the town and its details to fit the story than the fit the story into existing history. Though I stayed true to the atmosphere of the 1880s, I added those physical details I needed to fulfill the story line.

At this point I need to clarify the sawmill of the past, and research banking procedures from the 1880s in order to finish the story. I don't perceive any major changes happening in the story line.

(You can read the finished story, "The SomeWhen Murder," in the Central Coast Chapter of Sisters in Crime (SinC) anthology, *Somewhere in Crime*, available on Amazon Kindle.)

Unit 3: Story

"We are cups, constantly and quietly being filled. The trick is, knowing how to tip ourselves over and let the beautiful stuff out."

~Ray Bradbury

NOW THAT WE HAVE characters and settings, we need a story for them. Story is everywhere. It surrounds us on all sides, in everything we see and hear and experience. The smallest action, the softest word, contain their own story. Each picture tells a story. Every song. Each scent and taste. Every ray of sun and each raindrop. They all tell a story.

Recognizing stories is a process of learning **how to see and how to listen**. It's knowing how to find the unique in the ordinary, the amazing in the mundane. We can find stories in our own lives and the lives of our relatives and our friends. Even in the strangers around us. Possibilities are everywhere, if we learn how to find them.

But just because we can find the seeds of stories around us, it doesn't mean that there are full stories contained in them. Just like grain sown in the field, some story seeds will wither long before their details fully unfold. These 10 exercises will help you learn to see the story potential around you, and how to evaluate the viability of the seed idea.

Unit 3, Story: Contents

Lesson #1: The Story Statement

ALL STORIES START WITH an idea. Something triggers a thought in your mind and suddenly there's a character or a setting, an interesting scene, a theme or the inkling of a plot jumping up and down, shouting, "Write me! Write me!"

Then the fun begins. More characters appear. Alternate settings crop up. Twists worm their way into the plot, and subplots start adding depth and even more possibilities. You're pulled here, then there, then somewhere else. Your mind is working a mile a minute, trying to keep up and get it down on paper. It's hard enough to keep all this straight in the writing. It's even harder not to get lost in the details—to forget the original idea that started the adventure.

But **that idea is the reason for the story**. It's the seed from which the story grows and the foundation on which the story stands. If you forget that seed, if you lose it along the way, your story will have a tendency to wander, to focus on characters, events and themes that have no real connection or relevance to the original seed idea. We've all read stories that seem to lose focus partway through. We've all wondered at times, "Why did the author do that? It doesn't make sense." That's because the writer lost focus on the original seed idea. The foundation disappeared and so the story edifice collapsed.

It's bad enough to read a story like that. It's a tragedy to be in the middle of writing one that falls apart. One of the best ways to ensure we never lose sight of our original idea is to create a **Story Statement**, a one-sentence condensation of the story trigger. This is similar to the one-sentence "elevator pitch" that is so talked about today, but it is less refined. It is merely a statement of what enthralled you at the start, what piqued your interest enough to begin ideating and writing.

This is not always as easy as it seems. Often our original idea feels a bit unfocused if we try to put it into a succinct sentence. We're used to thinking in terms of completed plots and fully-rounded characters, and this statement is certainly not that polished. In fact, the fewer specific details, the better.

I've found that putting it into "What if…?" terms makes it easier to isolate the original seed idea from all the details and twists under which the imagination buries it.

In *The Novel Writer's Toolkit*, Mayer cites this example, Allan Folsom's seed idea for his novel, *The Day After Tomorrow*: "What if a man sitting in a Paris cafe sees someone who had played a significant role in his earlier life but whom he hadn't seen in twenty years?" As you can see, this is not a fully realized plot. Actually, it's not really a plot at all. Little detail is known except that there is a man in a cafe in Paris. Even those details could change in the writing. It could be a woman in a coffee shop in Los Angeles, and yet the seed idea is still there. It's the significant role played in early life, the twenty-year separation and the unexpected reunion that forms the basis of the story.

Another example of a "What if...?" story statement, from my suspense novel *Tangled Webs* (available on Amazon.com in print and digital format): "What if a woman was forced to live in the small town that hated her?" From my paranormal suspense novel *Proof of Identity*: "What if two people did have the same fingerprints?" And from my newly released suspense novel *Sins of the Past*: "What if someone in the Witness Protection Program was found?"

You can see that none of these "What If...?" statements limit you as the writer. In fact, they give almost limitless possibilities because of their open-endedness, the lack of specific details about characters and/or settings.

Of course, your original idea, i.e. the Story Statement, doesn't have to be expressed in a "What if...?" format. But it most often is the easiest way to formulate a "short-and-sweet" sentence about the seed of your story. Writing the Story Statement and pinning it up where you can see it as you write is an excellent way to keep yourself from wandering off the path when in the throes of crafting the twists and turns of your story.

Read: *The Novel Writer's Toolkit* (Mayer, 2003), Page 40 ("The Original Idea") to page 41, ending after 3rd full paragraph.

Read: *The 38 Most Common Mistakes in Fiction* (Bickham, 1992), Page 69 - 70, ending after 2nd full paragraph on page 70.

Exercise #1: The Simple Story Statement

(Purpose of Exercise: to practice creating story statements)

THINK UP POSSIBLE IDEAS for future stories and write **at least 10 Story Statements**. You can use the "What if...?" statement format or not, as you choose. If you can't think of 10 new ideas, try for at least six, and then do the rest from stories you have already written. Or even stories you have read. For further practice at a later date, if you want, continue with new ideas. Or use books you've read, or a volume of short stories, and write Story Statements for them, too.

Now set your timer for **15 MINUTES** and start writing.

Lesson #2: Expanding the Story Statement

IF YOU'RE JUST WRITING a short story, your one-sentence Story Statement should be enough to keep you fully on track. But a novel—and even a long short story—consists of many twists, turns, subplots, events and characters. Even with the short seed statement, it is still easy to get lost in the writing.

The Expanded Story Statement, though still a short "elevator-type" pitch, contains the necessary elements that will help keep your focus on the original story as you plot your tale. This statement contains:

1. the basic plot situation
2. the name of the main protagonist
3. the protagonist's story goal
4. the antagonist's name and goal
5. how the protagonist's goal opposes the main character

Seems like a lot to put into one little statement? It is, but it forms the basis for the actual elevator pitch you will need once your story is finished. And trust me, it is much easier to do this in the beginning, when the story is still in "seed" form, than afterwards when your mind is loaded down with minute details of characters, settings, plots and twists, subplots, etc.

While the Simple Story Statement is one sentence, often expressed as a question, the Expanded Story Statement consists of two-sentences. The first is a sentence sets up the situation and protagonist's name and goal. It is a statement, not a question. The second sentence can be formulated as a question or not, as you choose, but should contain the antagonists' name, goal and how it opposes the protagonist's goal.

Jack Bickham, on page 70 of *The 38 Most Common Mistakes in Fiction* (1992), uses one of his own stories as an example, the first in the Brad Smith espionage series (brackets mine): "Called back to duty [situation] by his former CIA masters, aging tennis star Brad Smith [name and identity] goes to Budapest to try to help a young woman tennis player escape that country [protagonist's goal]. But can he get her out when the CIA plot is foiled, he is alone [protagonist's desire and plan], and the UDBA [protagonist's identity] is onto his mission?"

Another example from my own *Tangled Webs*: "Forced back to her narrow-minded small town by her mother's will [situation], Lia Willett, a serial killer's daughter who suffers from partial amnesia [protagonist's name and identity], wants to live a quiet life until she can gain her inheritance and leave town [protagonist's goal]. But as danger swirls around her, will Detective Ross Gardner [antagonist's name and identity] find evidence to prove that, seventeen years earlier, Lia murdered a classmate [protagonist's desire and plan]?"

I found this statement extremely difficult to craft, because it was done after the book was written. All the minutia of the novel crowded in, wanting equal billing in the statement. I agonized about what to put in, and what to leave out. The statement would have been much easier to write before all the subplot "webs" had tangled up in the writing of the story.

Writing out the Expanded Story Statement will help you keep your eye on the main plot of your novel as you work, so you don't lose focus in the writing or get tangled up in the subplots. And it will help you craft an impressive and compelling elevator pitch once your book is done.

READ: *The 38 Most Common Mistakes in Fiction* (Bickham, 1992) Page 70 starting with the 3rd full paragraph, to page 71, ending after the 1st full paragraph.

Exercise #2 The Expanded Story Statement

(Purpose of Exercise: To learn to incorporate the basic plot into the story statement.)

WRITE AN EXPANDED STORY statement about a story you're working on, or choose one of the possible story statements you crafted in Exercise #1. Write the statement in 150 words or less—preferably less. Include the following in your statement:

First Sentence should contain:

1. The basic plot situation in which the story is to play.

2. The name and identity of the main plot character (protagonist).

3. That character's story goal.

Second Sentence/Question should contain:

4. The name of the primary opposition character (antagonist).

5. What this "villain" wants and how he/she opposes the main character.

Give yourself **15 MINUTES** to finish this exercise.

When you are done, look at your two main characters. Imagine what will happen to them during the course of the story physically, mentally, emotionally, spiritually. Then answer these questions. Who are they at the beginning of the story? Who are they at the end? How might those changes affect the flow of the story?

Now give yourself about **10 MINUTES** to make some notes on these characters for when you start writing the actual story.

Lesson #3: The What If? Game

"WHAT IF?" QUESTIONS ARE wonderful devices for triggering story ideas. Not sure what to write about? Just sit down and play "The What if...? Game," and you'll create a wonderful backlog of story ideas.

The basic "rule" for this game is to take something ordinary and give it a bit of a twist. It's a bit like brainstorming, in that it's open-ended and allows your imagination to stretch and be playful. Any answer is the right answer. There are no stupid ideas, no "right" or "wrong" ideas, only ideas that might lead to other ideas—and to great stories.

Don't judge any idea that occurs to you. Simply jot down each one as you think of it. You never know when an idea that is eminently unworkable will lead to one that forms the perfect major plot point, or is the ideal solution for resolving a major plot dilemma.

This game is based on asking, "What if (something) happens?" then goes on to refine the idea to make it a strong story statement. It does not include character names, desires and goals, though it may contain the kernel of those things. When refined, it becomes a story statement strong enough to form the framework for a fascinating, amusing, intriguing and/ or compelling story.

READ: *The Novel Writer's Toolkit* (Mayer, 2003), page 42 starting with the 3rd full paragraph, to page 43, ending after the 3rd full paragraph.

*Exercise #3: The What If? Game**

(Purpose of exercise: To learn how to find and refine story ideas)

SET YOUR TIMER FOR **15 MINUTES**. Write out at least 5 "What If...?" statements that could be the nuggets of 5 different stories.

Examples:

1) *What if a housewife realizes her life is empty and decides to change it?*

2) *What if a volcano erupted downwards instead of upwards?*

When you finish your 5 "What If...?" statements, go back and expand them to include more specific details that will hone the seminal ideas into story lines. Try to "twist" each idea just a bit out of the ordinary if you can.

Examples:

1) *What if a repressed housewife feels her husband doesn't love her and she gets a job as a pole dancer?*

2) *What if Mt. Pinatubo in the Philippines erupted downward into the Philippine Trench instead of into the atmosphere?*

If you finish before the timer dings, continue writing "What if...?" statements and refining each one.

Lesson #4: Multiple Story Possibilities

IT'S A BIG LEAP from original idea to story. Not all ideas will translate successfully into stories. And some rather poor ideas can often morph into compelling tales.

How do you know if an idea is "good enough" to actually become a story worth writing? It's difficult enough to write a story without being handicapped with an idea that won't support the story. Think of the idea, or Story Statement, as the foundation upon which you erect the tale. If the foundation is weak and falters, the story will collapse in upon itself. And you will have wasted weeks or even months of your time.

Expanding on the "What if...?" theme can help you discover how solid your foundation idea is, and even if there is more than one story contained in the idea. Actually, because story statements are purposely vague and open-ended, you often can find more than one good story from each statement. In fact, in my "What if? Writing Group," I have given my students the same story statement to start with, and each one wrote a completely different story from it. That's because our writing and our thought processes are informed by our lives. And since no one lives the exact same life in the exact same way, everyone's story, and everyone's way of telling that story, is different.

You should never be afraid to tell anyone your story idea (statement), because the story you tell from it will be uniquely your own. The direction your plot goes in depends on how you think, the events you create, the way you link those events together, and the kind of characters with which you populate your story.

As you ask your "What if...?" questions, keep in mind that you want to intrigue the reader. So, what "twists" can you add to the list of questions? What if things are not as they seem? What if new characters with opposing goals intrude? What if the geography changes? The genders? The occupations? And so on...

After you work through this lesson, you may discover a full plot being developed. Or you may find two, three or even more different directions your original idea might take. You might find that with a change of gender, occupation or geography, your story becomes something totally different. When you see such things happening, go with them and see where they lead you. It's always a thrill to be able to write more than one story from a single seed idea.

And if you discover that your original seed idea really goes nowhere, you can drop it in relief, knowing that you haven't wasted more than about 10 or 15 minutes of your time, as opposed to weeks or months of story or novel writing. Then you can simply ask "What if...?" once again with a new seed idea to start the idea-generating process all over again.

READ: *The Novel Writer's Toolkit* (Mayer, 2003), Page 46 ("Idea Does Not Equal Story") to the end of page 48, ending after last full paragraph.

*Exercise #4: Multiple Story Possibilities**

(Purpose of Exercise: To discover the story in the idea)

TAKE ONE OF THE expanded "What If...? Statements" from Lesson #3 and continue with your "What If?" questions to find the story in the idea.

Ex: Original expanded "What if... ?" Statement from Lesson #3:

"What If... a repressed housewife feels her husband doesn't love her and she gets a job as a pole dancer?"

Continuing "What If...?" Questions:

What if she gets in debt with the owner of the place?

What if the interest is structured so that she can never pay it off but doesn't realize it?

What if the owner makes her do private lap dances to pay off her debt?

What if the owner wants her to do full nude dancing?

What if the owner threatens her husband/children if she doesn't do what he says?

What if she falls in love with one of the customers?

What if the customer is an undercover vice cop?

What if the cop falls in love with her, too?

What if the club owner is in Witness Protection and the vice cop can't arrest him?

What if the cop and the housewife plan to run away together?

What if the owner finds out about their plans and threatens her children?

What if her husband finds out about her extracurricular job and threatens to divorce her, naming the club owner as corespondent?

What if the husband threatens the customer she's in love with?

What if the husband takes the children and disappears?

Etc, etc, etc...

As you can see, this is not plotting an actual story. It's merely letting your mind go in as many directions as it can with this one story idea. A lot of your "What If?" questions will lead nowhere. And some will go in directions you might never have consciously thought about.

Give yourself **15 MINUTES** for this exercise. Set your timer and begin writing!

When you have finished with your list of questions, go back over them and see which of them seem to work into a cohesive plot, one following the other. Do any of the ideas go off on another tangent, seem to point to a different story? Is there a way to twist the events even more?

Lesson #5: Stories From Prompts

STORY IDEAS ARE EVERYWHERE. We just have to learn to look for them, to be aware of our surroundings, what we see, hear, smell, touch and taste. Everything in life is a possible story if we are open enough to recognize it.

One great source for story ideas are prompts. A prompt is a word or phrase that starts your creative juices flowing. It gives you a starting place without limiting your creativity, or paralyzing you with a totally blank sheet of (real or virtual) paper. A prompt, also called an opening line or phrase, allows your imagination to free-associate and your subconscious to pick up on subtle clues and deeply buried ideas that have been waiting for release.

A good practice is to keep lists of things you see, hear, feel, smell and taste to use as prompts. You can also use snippets of sentences you overhear when you're in public places as writing prompts. Perhaps a phrase from someone passing by who is on a cell phone will spark an idea. Or a half-heard sentence from the next table when you're having lunch or dinner in a restaurant will set a train of thought racing. Or a partial line of dialogue from a TV show or movie will spark your interest. (This really works. A partial line of dialogue from a "Buffy" episode sparked an idea in me for a book and its title. The first page of the YA work-in-progress won first place for the novel category in the Lillian Dean Competition at the Central Coast Writers Conference in 2011.)

Often these phrases or sentence fragments can serve as the opening sentence of your piece as well as the idea for the story. I always keep a small notebook open on my table when I dine out, so I can jot down snippets of conversations to use at a later date. I might seem to be absorbed in the book I brought in with me (and at times I am), but my ears are always open to the sounds that surround me. I've garnered many ideas from half-heard phrases uttered at other tables.

Stories are all around us. Train yourself to be aware, to look and listen for the unusual, the unique, the intriguing. Not only will you gather a plethora of prompts to set your imagination in gear, but you also will deepen your appreciation of your surroundings and the people, animals and birds that populate your world. You also might want to check out my blog for some great ways to use photographs to spark story, setting and character ideas. (www.SusanTuttleWrites.com/womanof1000words)

READ: Write Away (George, 2004), Page 39 to page 40, ending after last full paragraph

Exercise #5: Stories from Prompts*

(Purpose of Exercise: To find stories in everyday objects and ideas)

CHOOSE ONE OF THE prompts below, then set your timer for **20 MINUTES** and begin writing your story.

1. Write a story about: A secret
   Start with: One thing kept running through her mind.

2. Write a story about: An object that has been lost
   Start with: They went into the garden after dinner.

3. Write a story about: Something you can't see
   Start with: I closed the door behind me.

4. Write a story about: Someone dangerous
   Start with: My father was away.

Lesson #6: Stories From the News

ANOTHER GREAT SOURCE OF ideas are news articles in newspapers, on radio and television and on the internet. Our world is filled with strange people and events and these things are perfect take-off points for stories.

Look for news stories that have unexplained events or weird occurrences, stories that leave you wondering, "Why?" Or asking, "How could anyone be so stupid?" Or saying, "I can't believed that happened. What in heaven's name were these people thinking?" These make the best news items from which to glean story ideas because the are, by nature, open to interpretation.

When you start looking for news stories like these, you'll be amazed at how many there are out there to mine for ideas. I found the stories for this exercise in one online session that took me about 10 minutes to find and note down (the list I use in class is actually longer by three items). Imagine how many story ideas you would have if you spent 10 minutes a day for just one month searching online news outlets. (For example, if you found only 5 news items a day for 30 days, you would have 150 news stories from which to work.) It would take a lot of time to write them all, especially since you can probably get more than one story idea from each of them.

Keep a notebook with you when you watch TV news casts and news-related programs (and when listening to radio news shows; NPR is a great resource), and jot down the gist of what happened. Be sure to also note the questions the stories raised in your mind when you heard them. (Don't ever make the mistake of thinking you'll remember them. By the time your day ends and you are free to think about what you heard, 99% of the time your thoughts will have moved on and your original question will be lost.) Cut out articles from local newspapers and news magazines to use as story sparkers. The airwaves and print media are filled with wonderful news items you can use as a base for story ideas.

READ: *Write Away* (George, 2004), Page 47 to the end of the first full paragraph on page 49.

*Exercise #6: Stories from the News**

(Purpose of Exercise: To write fiction stories based on actual events)

SET YOUR TIMER FOR **20 MINUTES** and write a story based on one of the following actual news stories (yes, they are all actual stories that appeared either online on in the newspaper, even #5). Be sure to use "What if…?" questions to twist the events and make it your own version of what happened and why.

1) A Royal Palace guard used his Facebook account to denigrate Kate Middleton because he claimed she "snubbed him" while visiting the palace. She gave him a brief wave while looking the other way. He

said she was stuck up and thought he was not good enough for her. He has been dismissed as one of the Royal Guards during the wedding procession, considered to be a high honor in Britain.

2) The government will regulate electronic cigarettes as tobacco products, even though they do not contain any tobacco. These electronic devices mimic the act of smoking and include nicotine, but do not emit the same odor or ash as traditional cigarettes.

3) A woman was mauled to death by a pack of four pit bulls that escaped from the fenced yard of a private home. A bystander tried to help, but was driven back into his car when one of the dogs came after him. A police officer shot and killed one dog; the rest have been take into custody. Authorities are attempting to determine if criminal charges can be brought against the dogs' owners, who were not home at the time of the attack.

4) The sub-atomic particle known as the Higgs boson may have been found in the world's largest atom smasher. In Standard Model Physics, the Higgs boson is also called the "God particle" because physicists theorize that it bestows mass on all other particles. Controversy continues to rage over whether the Higgs boson actually exists, or if this anomaly is another type of particle that is a result of new physics beyond the Standard Model.

5) A small town changed its name from But Tussle to Giggleswick for undisclosed reasons. Residents refuse to talk about the name change, and no one has moved out of town because of the switch.

Lesson #7: Story Ideas From Story Endings

ONE REALLY FUN WAY to jump-start your inner story-idea machine is to use the ending paragraphs of published stories. Anthologies of short stories are great sources for this story-generating technique.

They have to be stories you **have not yet read**. If you have read them, you will begin with pre-conceived notions about the events leading up to the ending paragraph and that will interfere with the smooth flow of your own ideas. The story will end up a hybrid of your ideas and the published author's story. So make sure you have not read any of the stories whose ending paragraphs you use for this exercise.

The purpose here is to work backward to tell the story of what happened that led to this particular ending. Since you don't know anything but the final few sentences, you have to craft the plot on your own, entirely from your imagination. You need to ask yourself, "How did this character come to this point in time? Where did he/she start from? What events occurred to bring about this conclusion, and how did the character change or grow throughout the story?"

Once you write the story up to the published ending, you can then craft your own ending. Which, of course, you will need to, because (all issues of plagiarism aside) although you began with a pre-written ending in mind, your characters and events will take you in a slightly— or even vastly—different direction. As the events, settings and characters become your own, the story's direction and theme will resonate with your view and the way you put your words and sentences together. The story will demand its own ending.

It's also fun to try to match the tone, mood and pacing of the published ending paragraph, especially if it's different from the way you usually write. If it doesn't work, you can always change it in the rewrite. But stretching yourself to try something new always adds to the depth and color of your writing. Whether you ever write that genre or use that tone, mood or pacing again, you will have gained from the experience and taken the lessons learned back to your regular writing.

READ: *Write Away* (George, 2004), Page 178-179

$Exercise$ #7: Story endings as Idea Sparkers

(Purpose of Exercise: To jump-start original story lines from the endings of published stories)

READ THE FOLLOWING ENDING paragraphs of these published works. Then pick one and write the story that leads up to the ending. Try to match the tone, mood and pacing of the given paragraph. When you reach the end of your story, write your own concluding paragraph.

These paragraph endings are all from Central Coast authors who I know, great writers every one of them, and are used with their permission.

The final one is from "Coffin of Silence," a story I wrote originally using the ending paragraph of a story by Janice Booth. Of course, the ending paragraph here is the one that ends my story, not hers. "Coffin of Silence" appeared in the Summer 2012 issue of the now-defunct *The Feathered Flounder*, an online literary magazine.

Don't spend any time evaluating which paragraph to choose. Read through them and select the one you are most drawn to at first glance. Then set your timer for **25 MINUTES** and start writing.

A) He placed the flower behind her left ear, and as they drew near to kiss, he thought to himself that she was probably right.
(From: *The Curse of the Crimson Dragon*, by Tony Piazza: www.authortonypiazza.wordpress.com)

B) And that is how I ended up here, my friends, drinking in the shadows, seeking out the company of common sinners like myself. You speak of your woman, the lady who destroyed your soul, or who poured her love into you as though you were a holy chalice. My story ends as well. I am here to confess that I destroyed mine.
(From: "The Priest's Tale" by Anne Schroeder: http://anneschroederauthor.blogspot.com/; www.readanneschroeder.com)

C) She glanced at Brian as he peeked at her over the top of the newspaper. Caitland would hate the pun, she thought, but Brian was the best male she ever got. It was the Threepenny Opera all over. Get your money every Friday, happy endings are the rule.
(From: *Gambling For Good Mail* by Evelyn Cole: www.evelyn-cole.com)

D) I nodded. "Yes. Some kind of Robin Hood. I don't know if he's the good kind or the bad kind." I put four dollars in the register to pay for the card. "But I'll make sure he pays me when I see him again."
(From: *Sherwood Ltd.* by Anne Allen: www.annerallen.blogspot.com)

E) He slumped into the corner of the booth as the doctor held his chin and sewed the flaps of skin together. "That'll hurt tomorrow," he said cleaning the needle and putting it into his bag. "You the one we sent for?"
(From *Wake of the Liar* by Mark Arnold: https://www.smashwords.com/books/view/93948s)

E) I wonder if there is another access to the storage area. With my luck the coding system is a series of 0's and 1's and only a computer hacker could find the back door and the password.
(From: "Grieving Daughter, Dying Mother Journal," By Debra Davis Hinkle, in *Tears to Laugher: Embracing The Future Without Forgetting The Past* by Debra Davis Hinkle and Jim Leonard: www.kritiquekritics.com; www.kritiquekritics.com/tearstolaughter)

F) Anyway, I'm on my own now, free to read, sleep and think as I wish. That's the situation at the Men's Colony, another sort of desert, a place of isolation and contemplation, the solace broken only when I allow it to happen, when I focus on my constant companion, the ringing in my ears and know I am not alone.
(From "A Solitary Silence," by Paul Fahey, published in Sugar Mule, Issue #10, http://www.marclweber.com/sugarmule/frame10.htm)

G) The laddering moonlight had shifted. Blood-dark shadows now slashed across the bed where they lay alone, side by side, phantom nails impaling her breast, her belly, pinning her life to the mattress. She couldn't move. Eyes burning, she lay staring at the dark ceiling, drowning in silence, waiting for daylight to free her. She could still taste cold iron on her tongue.

(From: "Coffin of Silence," by Susan Tuttle: www.SusanTuttleWrites.com This is my ending paragraph from a story I wrote using as inspiration the ending paragraph of a story written by the instructor, Janice Booth. I was the only one in the class who matched the tone of Janice's work.)

Lesson #8: Story and the Human Psyche

ACTION CARRIES THE READER through the story, but story really is about characters. They strive, fail, pick themselves up again, strive some more, fail again, continue the process and eventually overcome—something.

Maybe the characters don't reach their stated goal. Perhaps they find a better goal. Or they might fail in the end but learn something important about themselves, something more important than the goal itself.

Whatever happens, they learn and they grow. If they don't, what's the point of writing the story? Why would anyone want to read it? Even the most entertaining, pure escapism stories still give the reader a sense of fulfillment, a satisfaction that comes from watching someone just like themselves overcome an obstacle and become more than they were at the beginning.

Choosing the right personality for our characters helps our stories come alive. Sometimes when a story isn't working it might be because we have the wrong personality types in the lead roles. It's amazing, when you switch character types, how the story itself can change.

I'm not talking about individual character traits here, the quirks that give our characters interest. I'm talking about the basic personality types that have been identified by psychologists. A good, basic knowledge of how these different personality types view the world can help us choose the right person to carry out our plots.

Basically, people can be separated into two main categories: Introverts and Extroverts. Each type can be either Stable or Unstable, and each has its own specific way of viewing the world, processing information, thoughts, ideas, feelings and events, and their own process of making decisions. Each type will have a unique effect on your story, depending on which ones you choose for your protagonist and antagonist.

So we have:

Stable Introverts (Thinking Types);

Unstable Introverts (Intuitive Types);

Stable Extroverts (Sensation Types);

Unstable Extroverts (Feeling Types).

Each type processes thoughts, ideas, feelings and events in specific ways.

Stable Introverts are also called Thinking Types. They are thinkers. They take their time, consider all the options, make rational decisions based on facts. They are meticulous immovable mountains that can't be rushed.

Unstable Introverts are called Intuitives. For them, the future is everything. They lay aside money for their retirement, make long-range plans for "someday" trips, and live with their eyes on tomorrow. Today is just something to get through so they can reach the perfect future that awaits them—someday. It rarely occurs to them that tomorrow never comes; by the time it arrives, it's already today.

Stable Extroverts are Sensation Types. They concentrate on "The Now" and live for today. "Carpe diem" is their motto. They rarely think past the next few days, and certainly aren't concerned with some far-off fantasy called retirement. They are often thought of as scatterbrained and impulsive, but they can be exciting to be around and make great friends because they will drop whatever they are doing at a moment's notice whenever you ask.

Unstable Extroverts are Feeling people. They live in the emotional past. They hang onto slights and grudges and often end up bitter and angry. They judge all thoughts and actions and other people by what happened in the past. They are closed to change and growth.

Becoming familiar with these four main personality types can help you choose the right character personalities for your stories, so they truly come alive.

Exercise #8: Character Traits and the Human Personality (Psyche)*

(Purpose of exercise: To understand the basic human personality types from which characters are drawn)

THERE ARE FOUR PARTS to this exercise, designed to help you understand the impact of each personality type on your story. It will take just over an hour to complete. Read each part in order as you do the exercise. **Resist the tendency to read ahead**. Carefully consider the exact impact each type has on the scenes you write.

Part I: Create a character based on the Stable-Introvert (thinking) Type and write a short action scene where he/she must take charge, solve a problem, win an argument, overcome an obstacle, etc. (Ex: a bank robbery, a car crash, etc.) Make it as exciting as you can and still be true to the Stable-Introvert personality type.

Set your timer for **20 MINUTES** and write!

Part II: When you have finished Part I, recreate the main character from the scene to fit the Unstable-Introvert (intuitive) personality type. Now time yourself for **15 MINUTES** and rewrite the exact same scene as above, substituting the Unstable Introvert for the Stable. When you have finished, analyze the scene. What changed because of the change in personality type? What couldn't happen because of the change? What happened because of it? Was the outcome the same or different? Is the story veering in another direction? Which scene do you feel is better, more exciting, deeper in meaning?

Part III: Again, with **15 MINUTES** on the timer, recreate the same scene, this time with the main character drawn as a Stable-Extrovert (sensation) Type. What has to change because of this personality type? Where is the story going now? Is this a better, worse or merely different direction than the first two?

Part IV: Yes, you guessed it. This time rewrite the same scene, with an Unstable-Extrovert (feeling) Type in the main character's place. Give yourself **15 MINUTES** to make the necessary changes, and when you have finished, analyze what changed in the action and interactions, what impact this personality type had on the resolution—or non-resolution—of the problem.

By analyzing how each personality type impacts the same scene, you can discover which works best within the confines of the story, which personality is the most exciting, engaging, unique, thought-provoking, etc., to carry the plot line forward to the end.

If you do this exercise with your story's pivotal scene and main characters, you will discover which personality types best fit the story and will be most interesting to the reader. And it may lead your story into areas you hadn't even considered.

Lesson #9: Story Ideas From Life

NOVELS BEGIN WITH AN idea that inspires the author to write it. And while stories are all around us, they are also within us. Our own lives can serve as inspiration for some really fantastic stories.

Oh, but your life is boringly average, you say? There just isn't anything interesting about it, certainly not enough to sustain an idea for even flash fiction, much less a short story or a novel.

I beg to differ. No matter how ordinary our lives may seem (and believe me, mine is as ordinary as they come), they still contain the seeds of countless stories. That's because as writers we **fictionalize** real life, adding twists, turns, tension and conflict that didn't happen in real life. We expand and contract facts and timelines, juicing it up, if you will. Then we stir in a dollop or two of creative imagination so that the story no longer matches reality, but merely uses reality as a springboard into the world of make-believe.

Once you get used to seeing the events, experiences, thoughts and conversations in your life—and those of your relatives and friends, too—as springboards, you'll begin to see nuggets everywhere you look, nuggets that can grow into short stories, novellas and novels. The main thing to remember is that you are using these events and experiences **only as the seed idea**. The plant that grows from this seed, irradiated with the power of your imagination, will be unique in and of itself, having little in common with the actuality on which it is based.

If people can guess what event, experience or conversation you based your story on, then you didn't change it enough. It will linger on the outskirts of creative non-fiction (the term used today for memoir and biography), never quite stepping over the border into full fiction. And full fiction is the desired end point, here—a story that is a wholly fictionalized, fanciful version of what just, maybe, perhaps might have happened… if only. Your fiction story will resemble the base reality as much as the James Bond movies resemble the James Bond novels by Ian Fleming. If you aren't familiar with that dichotomy, rent a video and then read Ian Fleming's book by the same name. You'll be astounded.

This is where your ability to twist reality out of kilter by asking and answering, "What if…?" truly comes in handy. And once you learn to do it well, you'll never run out of stories from your ordinary, normal, boring, everyday life.

Exercise #9: Mining Your Life for Story Ideas

(Purpose of Exercise: To understand how to mine our own lives for story ideas)

FOR EACH OF THE following, write out an idea that could be used to develop into a story or novel. You are not writing the story, only **the idea that could form a story** based on these experiences. Remember to continually ask, "What if...?" as you work on the ideas. Set your timer for **30 MINUTES** and start writing.

1) An idea based on personal experience

2) An idea about something that might have happened during a personal experience

3) An idea based on a philosophical conclusion about life as a result of a personal experience

4) An idea from a personal experience based on something you saw or heard

5) An idea based on your family history

6) An idea based on something a friend or relative suggested

7) An idea based on a strong feeling you have against something

8) An idea based on a strong feeling you have for something

9) An idea based on a current event or news story that touches your life in some way

10) An idea based on a chance incident that happened to you

11) An idea based on a burning desire to experience something you have never experienced

12) An idea based on a change of manners and mores in society that affects your life in some way

13) An idea based on the introduction of a new invention that affects your life in some way

14) An idea based on social upheaval that affects your life in some way

15) An idea based on a strong interest of yours in a particular business or industry

Lesson #10: Testing Story Viability

ONE OF THE GREATEST tragedies that can happen to a writer, other than losing the only copy of a manuscript when the computer crashes, or it's left on a bus, cab or train seat, is to be halfway through writing a long story, novella or novel and have it fall apart. So much time wasted, so much hope crushed. If it happens, it can often be enough to make a writer give up.

There are many reasons why stories fall apart partway through. The writer loses interest and the writing feels stale. The plot stalls and nothing can get it restarted. The characters are cardboard cutouts with no real life in them. The story doesn't really go anywhere, it just sits like a bump on a log. The settings are mundane, not at all inspiring. The plot twists don't lead anywhere a writer would want to go, much less a reader. The writer would rather be grocery shopping, shoveling snow, changing the oil in the car—anything but writing that stupid story!

The majority of the time, these things occur because the story was **not truly viable from the beginning**. Webster defines viable as: "Born alive and so developed physically as to be normally capable of living." When we apply this definition to a story idea, we mean that the idea itself must be vital and alive enough to sustain interest and excitement for the many weeks, months and sometimes years it takes to write it.

It's almost impossible to breathe life back into a story that is born half-dead. As writers we must believe in the idea, be passionate about the theme and/or message contained in the story idea. We must be invigorated by the company of the characters—all of them, even the bad guys and the incidental ones.

But it's not easy to evaluate the viability of a new idea. By its very nature, new ideas are exciting and invigorating. They make our eyes sparkle, our synapses fire, our fingers tap out words on tables and countertops. Riding high on the euphoria of "The New Idea," we plunge into the writing without stopping to evaluate just how new or unique this idea is. Is there enough excitement to sustain extended close contact? Are the twists and turns intriguing enough to keep pushing us around corners? And is the purpose, theme or message strong enough to withstand the tedium of long hours at the computer, typing and doing research?

It's important to stop, before firing up the word processing program and sitting down at the keyboard, put on your "Stable Introvert" hat and evaluate the idea. When you look at the idea rationally and consider all its merits, you may find that it really isn't novel material. Or even novella material. It might hold only a short story's worth of effort. Or not be worth any effort at all.

Remember, even a short story can require weeks of work—eating, drinking and sleeping your story, as it were. It's truly a tragedy to waste time writing a story that will only be tossed aside after weeks or months of work, when a few minutes of evaluation could free you up to write a truly viable and exciting story.

Exercise #10: Testing the Story Idea for Viability

(Purpose of Exercise: To learn how to determine whether a story is worth writing before beginning to write.)

CHOOSE <u>ONE</u> OF THE ideas from Exercise #9 and complete the following list, answering as completely as you can. Evaluate what first excited you about the idea, what your message/theme is, how strong your commitment to writing this story is. Set your timer for **15 MINUTES** and evaluate your idea in depth to decide if it is a story you want to spend your precious time working on for the next few weeks or months.

1) My idea came from…

2) My idea is (Story Statement)...

3) Write your intention in one sentence. Start with: My intention is to write a novel about…

4) State your attitude toward this idea in one sentence. Start with: This is based on my strong belief that…

5) Explain why your attitude is clear, strong and meaningful.

6) Write your statement of purpose for this novel in one sentence. Start with: My purpose for this novel is to…

7) Does your statement of purpose point to the direction this novel must take?

8) Are you qualified from personal experience to write this novel?

9) Are you willing to do the research necessary to write this novel?

10) Are you willing to spend at least 6 months or more writing this one story?

11) Are you willing to do the promotion and marketing that selling this story or novel necessitates?

Examples From My Class Work

AGAIN, THESE EXAMPLES ARE taken from my in-class writings and are presented only to give you an idea of how each exercise might look like.

Lesson #3: The What If? Game

Part A: Simple What If? Statements

What If... a local grocery store sold hot beer?

What if... someone invented a drug that made everyone a genius?

What if... a company invented a way to colonize the ocean floor?

What if... a steroid altered the lifecycle of bed bugs?

What if... a woman had seven babies in seven years without ever having sex?

What if... Jesus returned as a talk show host?

What if... every time the phone rang it was bad news?

What if... the cure for cancer caused a major mutation in humanity?

Part B: Expanded What If? Statements

1) What if Trader Joe's grocery store sold an all natural beer that is only palatable when heated to 120 degrees?

2) What if a local housewife with a cooking show, who loves to experiment with cooking, inadvertently invented a drug that made everyone who ate her food a mathematics genius?

3) What if the Serta Mattress Company found a way to colonize the ocean floor in the Atlantic between America and Europe, which interrupts the shipping lanes?

4) What if an athletic trainer altered the steroid he gave his athletes so it migrated into skin cells that were then eaten by bed bugs, and the bed bugs mutated into human-eating monsters?

5) What if a young drug addict girl gave birth to seven babies in seven years without having sex, and the local media caught the story and took it global?

6) What if God, in the person of the risen Christ, returned to Earth and bought a TV station so He could host his own TV talk show called The Big Picture?

7) What if every time the phone rang in a US Senator's office, someone the Senator knew died a violent death?

8) What if a scientist discovered a cure for cancer that mutated people into nitrogen-breathing beings?

Lesson #4: Multiple Story Possibilities

This is from a story I am working on. I have the opening, but little concept of how the story will unfold. To find the story possibilities, I used this lesson to explore possible story lines.

Opening: The environment has been destroyed and martial law reigns. Janna, whose father was a dissident, comes to Tom's house because her 16-year-old brother Billy has been arrested and imprisoned for treason. They argue and before she can leave an earthquake hits. Janna is deeply cut and bleeding profusely. Tom is also injured, but he is determined to get Janna help. He assists her along the street to the nearest aid station.

From here I worked a series of What If? statements to see where the story might go, and when I finished I chose the one that appealed most to me (#1) and expanded that statement with more What If? possibilities.

1) What if: When they reach the aid station, Janna is refused help. She has to go to a special aid station on the city perimeter for treatment.

2) What if: Soldiers intercept them and arrest Janna and take her away.

3) What if: Neighbors take Janna and Tom in, minister to them and hide them.

4) What if: Janna dies on the way and Tom is arrested for her murder.

5) What if: Janna's brother escapes jail because of the earthquake, then finds and kills Tom because he thinks Tom hurt Janna?

6) What if: Janna loses consciousness before they get to the secondary aid station?

7) What if: The Commander sees Janna and takes her into protective custody and imprisons Tom?

8) What if: They get treated at the aid station and then are evicted from the town and have no protected shelter from the environment.

9) What if: Billy's fellow dissidents break through the barriers to rescue Janna and Tom?

My choice to expand:

1) What if: When they reach the aid station, Janna is refused help. She has to go to a special aid station on the city perimeter for treatment.

a) What if: Janna loses consciousness on the way.

b) What if: a friendly doctor helps Janna by treating her with techniques forbidden to perimeter dwellers.

c) What if: Tom recovers first and moves into a newly constructed apartment for the upper class and then has Janna move in with him.

d) What if: the military police arrest Janna because she doesn't have a resident permit.

e) What if: the Commander wants to break her spirit and destroy her bother, because he had been humiliated by her father?

f) What if: the Commander has already sent Billy to the concentration camp in the desert.

g) What if: Tom has to choose between his safe life in the city and rescuing Janna from the Commander.

h) What if: Tom chooses to rescue Janna and both must leave the city.

i) What if: Tom and Janna decide to try to rescue Billy from the camp.

j) What if: Tom and Janna have no weapons or gear as they travel across the country toward the camp.

k) What if they share the little they do have with two brothers who have been injured, helping them stay alive.

l) What if: What if they run into a wild group who sacrifice women to their evil god.

m) What if: the men capture Janna and prepare to sacrifice her.

n) What if: Tom tries to rescue her and fails.

o) What if: the two brothers meet up with Tom and help him rescue Janna.

p) What if the four stay together as they continue across the country.

q) What if: Janna finds herself pregnant. (etc. etc)

Lesson #5: Stories From Prompts

Write About A Lost Object (Prompt: They went into the garden after dinner.)

They went into the garden after dinner. Kristina's long skirt swept the cobbles, gathered the fallen leaves beneath its hem. Robert held her arm against his side, warming her with his body heat, since she hadn't stopped to fetch a shawl. Stars glittered like ice chips above, lit by a full round moon that shone blue-white against its ebony background. The misty umbra surrounding the disk foretold a turn of weather by morning.

"What do you mean, you don't have it?" Robert murmured to her as they passed the Abernathys. Cecilia nodded to Kristina and smiled and Kristina cursed the night shadows that hid her fear from the world.

"I told you, I lost it," she said, working hard to keep her voice steady.

"Where?" He pressed on her hand as he uttered the gutteral word and Kristina winced.

"If I knew where it wouldn't be lost, would it?" She took a deep breath, hoping the logic would soften him. Vain hope.

"How could you have been so careless?' Robert steered her to a far corner and pulled her around to face him. "You knew what was at stake. How could you possibly have let it out of your sight?"

"I'm sorry. Robert, please." Kristina twisted in his hands, sure she would bear bruises by morning. "You're hurting me."

"I'll do more than hurt you, Kristina. We have to find it. Where were you when you first realized it was missing?"

"On the train. Leaving Bern. It was in my hatbox when I left the hotel, but when I opened the box in the compartment, it was gone. It's nothing I did, Robert!" she cried when he lifted his hand, fingers curled into a fist. His ring caught the moonlight and fractured it like broken glass. "Someone stole it, somehow. Please, I'm sorry."

"You stupid fool," Robert said. He grabbed her hand and twisted it, took her to her knees in the garden where the rose thorns snagged the silk of her dress. "I never should have trusted you."

"No, you shouldn't have," Kristina said.

Her quiet voice rang in the stillness. Robert's head jerked up. Kristina slid the small stiletto from her ankle sheath and jabbed upward, catching Robert between his ribs, beneath his heart. He folded down over her and she eased him to a sprawl against the garden's stone fence. Then she searched his pockets, found the small black book which she put in her reticule, and rose.

"I may have lost the map you needed to reach the tomb first, Robert," she said, staring into his dying eyes, "but I've completed my mission. I have the locations of all your encampments, thanks to your little book. Our consortium will be victorious. The Golden Fleece will be ours!"

Lesson #6: Stories From the News

News Story: Regulating Electronic Cigarettes

"But they're not cigarettes," Clara said. "How can they regulate them as if they were?"

"Ah," the professor said. "That is the point at hand. What are the moral implications of the government regulating such things?"

Stern picked up the latest electronic gadget his brother had sent him: an electronic cigarette. Powered by four button batteries and containing a renewable capsule of nicotine-laced fiber, the slim cylinder mimicked the action of smoking without emitting a traditional cigarette's stench or leaving ashes and unsightly butts around. The class sat up in their seats, alert for once.

"They do contain nicotine, right?" Alex asked. "So, I suppose you could say they are a drug delivery system. Drugs are already regulated, aren't they? So why not this?"

"But they're regulating it as a tobacco product," Stern said, and watched half the class frown in obvious confusion.

"And they only regulate illegal drugs—or at least try to," Clara said. "Alcohol isn't regulated and it's as much a drug as nicotine."

"All they want is money," Jennifer said, her voice raining down from the last row of the tier. "Regulation means taxes which means money. That's all they care about."

"It feels like Big Brother to me," Clara said. "Doesn't that scare anybody?"

"You don't like it, don't use them," Alex said, shrugging his shoulders. "What's the big deal?"

"The big deal is, where will it stop? Right, professor?" Jennifer stood up. "Pretty soon they'll find some spurious reason to slap a regulation on eye glasses, because they help you see better. And beach balls, because they're lighter than baseballs and harder to throw any distance."

"And what about microwaves?" Paul added, sitting up on his desktop. "You could kill a person with a microwave, not just your dinner. That could be regulated, too. Taxed murder."

The class laughed, though half of them looked disturbed over the direction in which the dialogue was heading.

"And the washer and dryer, for using water and power," voices piped up all over the room, "and the lawnmower for releasing chlorophyll scents into the air, and fabric dye because your neighbor might be allergic to the color."

Laughter rang throughout the room. Then the doors burst open and uniformed men marched in, brandishing weapons.

"Nobody move!" shouted a tall man sporting a chest full of military medals. "You're all being detained. Come with us."

"Detained?" Clara asked. "What for?"

"For having original thoughts. There's a huge tax on that. Plus you've had some good ideas. The government has been running out and we need new blood." He turned to Professor Stern. "Thanks for your help, sir. As promised, we won't regulate your class. Not yet, anyway."

Lesson #8: Story and the Human Psyche

This is a partial example from what I wrote in class, containing only the first two Human Personality types.

Stable Introvert: George had just returned from a late lunch that overcast winter afternoon, the same peanut butter and marshmallow sandwich and apple juice he'd had everyday for fifteen years, when the shooting started. His pen stopped moving and his heart began to race, but he kept his head lowered and forced his mind to think.

Where were the shots coming from, exactly? How close to him? It was a huge bank, with vaulted ceiling and marble walls off which the noise reverberated. George had watched enough TV shows to know that sudden moves—not that he was ever given to sudden anything—attracted unwanted and often dangerous attention. So, he sat and listened and worked hard to keep his breathing steady as screams and shouts rained down around him.

Most of the melee seemed to be concentrated off to his left, near the head teller's station. George laid down his pen and turned his head, saw three masked men with what looked like machine guns herding customers and floor reps toward the wall. A fourth man frisked the guard's body where it sprawled on the floor near the main entrance doors. George couldn't tell if Adam had been hurt, but he thought yes. No one could lay that still and still retain consciousness. The felon stood, walked to the entry doors and locked them with Adam's keys.

No one had yet looked his way, to where his desk stood half-hidden behind a grouping of potted palms. He carefully, with small, precise movements, gathered the loan papers spread out on the desktop and slid them into a bottom drawer. Then he slowly slithered off the chair onto the cold stone floor.

What to do? One of the robbers stood beside Carrie, the head teller, as she shoveled money into a canvas sack. George could tell, from the way the masked man kept glancing at the station phone, that he was alert for any red lights that would signal a telephone in use. George daren't pick up his receiver to call the police. And he didn't have a panic button beneath his desk.

He lay watching two of the thieves move among the customers, removing watches, rings, jewelry and wallets. The third robber prodded Carrie to the next station, where she opened the money drawer and began emptying it. The fourth man kept sentry at the main doors, sweeping his machine gun around the vast room, ready to open fire at the least provocation.

George quietly slithered along the floor on his belly, heading for the maintenance room. The row of potted plants helped hide his movements. He slowly inched open the maintenance room door and rolled inside. What now? He asked himself. What could he do here that would help the situation? He still couldn't phone for help; the red light would give him away. And there was no panic button in this room.

Then an idea struck and he ran to the far wall, opened a small metal door, pulled a switch and plunged the entire building into darkness.

Unstable Introvert: George had already pulled out two hanks of hair over the discrepancy in the loan documents—they always gave him the screwed up ones, wanting to see how much more he could screw them up—when the shooting started. He jumped a foot in his seat and tossed his pen into the air, screeching like a schoolgirl, then cowered among the palms that half-hid him from view. Four men in masks had invaded the huge bank. Their shouts reverberated in George's head, making it impossible for him to think.

"Everybody!" the tallest one shouted. "Over here, against the wall. Move it! Come on you," he grabbed one of the floor officers, yanked her up from her chair and shoved her toward the side wall, "move your ass."

Two of the men guarded the hostages while one forced head teller Carrie to open and empty the cash drawers, one by one. The fourth man hit Adam, the elderly security guard, on the back of his head. The old man dropped to the floor with an audible thunk, and George winced. Then the robber bent over Adam's body and extracted a set of keys which he used to lock the main entry doors.

My God! George thought. We're trapped in here! They'll kill us all!

He shoved up from the chair and lurched into his desk. It skidded a few inches on the slick marble, making a high-pitched squeak. One of the robbers turned and saw him where he cowered half-hidden behind a row of potted palms. He crossed to George with swift strides and grabbed the front of George's shirt.

"You think you're immune, asshole?" he growled. "You want me to shoot you?"

"N-n-no," George stammered, his knees buckling.

Afterword

"Who wants to become a writer? And why? Because it's the answer to everything. ... It's the streaming reason for living. To note, to pin down, to build up, to create, to be astonished at nothing, to cherish the oddities, to let nothing go down the drain, to make something, to make a great flower out of life, even if it's a cactus."

~Enid Bagnold

YOU HAVE NOW WORKED through the three key aspects of writing fiction—Character, Setting and Story—and have in hand a series of exercises you can repeat over and over as you need to or desire. These lessons form the foundation blocks of your stories, the base on which all your other skills will build and grow.

You have learned how to create characters who are fascinating, flawed and filled with vision and desire. Characters readers will want to read about. As you've seen, taking the time to create fully rounded characters can be difficult at times, and time consuming, but well worth it in the end.

And you know now how to craft settings and landscapes that will draw readers into your tale, settings that enhance their reading experience and inform them every step of the way. Whether your settings are homes, offices, factories, oceans, forests, caverns or worlds on the other side of our galaxy, you have strategies to help you create places that will live in the minds of your readers.

Finally you learned where to find the stories that will give your settings a reason for being and your characters motivation to do what they must, challenges to overcome and battles to win. With these elements in place, you have a story readers will want to read.

These are the three key elements of fiction writing: Character, Setting and Story. But they're only the beginning of your journey.

Where do you go from here? How do these elements come together into a cohesive whole? What comes next in the listing of the 12 major skills needed to unlock the stories that reside deep within your psyche?

Point of View.

Point of View (POV) is one of the most difficult concepts to master in the art of fiction and creative nonfiction writing, mainly because it has so many subtle nuances. Even well-known, best-selling authors can switch POVs without realizing it. And even when they are subtle, POV deviations can pull readers out of the flow of the story and diminish the reading experience for them.

In *Write It Right Workbook #2: Point of View (POV)* you will discover **15 lessons** to help you navigate the murky waters of Point of View. You'll learn the difference between straight, emotional omniscient and classic omniscient POV, and understand the strengths and drawbacks of each one. You'll gain experience in first, second and third person POVs, and work through the differences in shifting, close and alternating POVs. You will learn how to identify which character can best tell your story, and how to remain in that character's viewpoint consistently.

And the journey continues...

Workbook #3: Plot, Dialogue will teach you how to formulate plots that will draw readers through your stories, plots that enhance the reading experience and deepen the message imparted in the struggle to find success. And you'll learn the essential elements of effective dialogue, dialogue that sounds natural while it fulfills the six critical ingredients of dynamic dialogue necessary for every story.

Workbook #4: Scenes, Style/Voice contains lessons and exercises that will help you understand the 9 different types of scene structures and how each affects the rhythm and pacing of your stories. The Unit on Style/Voice will help you develop your own unique writing style, a clear, consistent voice that will stand out among all the others and be readily recognizable as yours alone.

Workbook #5: Conflict/Tension, Subplot will show you how to create and sustain the tension that keeps readers turning pages through 9 tension-filled exercises. The 9 strategies contained in the unit on Subplot will help you add depth and dimension to your work by weaving fascinating subplots into your main stories. In this workbook, you will also learn the secret to creating an effective and compelling series that satisfies readers as it pulls them through one volume to the next.

Workbook #6: Beginnings, Endings gives you 8 different formats each for opening your story and for ending your story. In Brilliant Beginnings you will also learn how to polish that all-important first sentence/first paragraph/first page so that readers are compelled to continue reading. And in Extraordinary Endings, you will learn the secrets to choosing the proper ending for whatever story you write, so that readers smile and say, "I'm so glad I read that!"

Look for the entire *Write It Right: Exercises to Unlock the Writer in Everyone* workbook series on Amazon.com in print format. Each individual unit will eventually be available in digital format in the Kindle store, but the workbooks themselves are available only in print because I feel that is the most useful format for serious writers. You can have the book open on your desk as you work on the exercises either by hand of on the computer, and not have to keep switching from one window to another to check on the exercise parameters or re-read the lesson as you work.

Thank you for purchasing this Workbook. I hope you find it helpful on your writing journey. If you do, please take the time to write a review on Amazon.com, since that's where most of my sales come from. In this digital age of social media, it's reader reviews that best help sell books. As does word of mouth, so be sure to tell all your writer friends about the *Write It Right* series, so they can also benefit from the program.

Also, if you'd like, please drop by my website (www.SusanTuttleWrites.com) and leave a comment or two about the photos and story/character/setting ideas you'll find (Category: Woman of 1,000 Words), the weekly writing prompts that post every Wednesday (Category: Write Over The Hump), about the *Write It Right* program, or any other writing subject that comes to mind. Or email me at aim2write@yahoo.com. I'd love to hear from you.

Susan's Books

I NEVER THOUGHT, WHEN I started to write my own stories, that one day I would produce an entire series of workbooks on how to write fiction (and creative nonfiction, because these days that genre needs to be structured in the same manner as fiction). I never thought it even when I started teaching fiction writing. Getting my novels out was my main goal. But life has a way of guiding you down paths you don't even know are there, and this is where I've been led.

What follows is a listing of the books I have out in either print or ebook format, or both—and those in process of being readied for print/e-format. The *Write It Right Workbooks* head the list, but I'm also adding in my fiction titles at the end (suspense and paranormal suspense) in case you might like to take a peek at them, too (all available on Amazon.com and Amazon Kindle). I think they're pretty great, but then, as the author, I'll admit I'm a bit prejudiced.

My hope is that my *Write It Right Workbooks* will help unlock the talent and amazing stories that reside in each and every one of you. Happy writing!

Susan's Nonfiction Books

Write It Right Workbooks available from Amazon Print:

Workbook #1: Units 1, 2, 3: Character, Setting, Story

Workbook #2: Unit 4: POV*

Workbook #3: Units 5, 6: Plot, Dialogue*

Workbook #4: Units 7, 8: Scenes, Style/Voice, Conflict*

Workbook #5: Units 9, 10: Conflict/Tension, Subplot*

Workbook #6: Units 11, 12: Beginnings, Endings*

Write It Right Individual Units available from Amazon Kindle:

Volume 1: Character

Volume 2: Setting

Volume 3: Story

Volume 4: Point of View (POV)

Volume 5: Plot*

Volume 6: Dialogue*

Volume 7: Scenes*

Volume 8: Style and Voice*

Volume 9: Conflict/Tension*

Volume 10: Subplot*

Volume 11: Brilliant Beginnings*

Volume 12: Extraordinary Endings*

*Coming in late Summer, 2014

Susan's Fiction Books

Suspense

Tangled Webs
Sins of the Past

Paranormal Suspense

Proof of Identity

Coming Soon:

A Matter of Identity, historical suspense

Piece By Piece, adult suspense

Obsession, adult suspense

Stealing Shyon, adult fantasy

The Skylark Series: paranormal detectives

The Somewhen Murder

Dead Ringer

Someone Else's Eyes

Destany's Daughter, a paranormal YA / Adult fantasy series

CPSIA information can be obtained
at www.ICGtesting.com
Printed in the USA
LVOW03s1021220716
497382LV00011B/148/P